WHY FORGIVENESS IS IMPORTANT

Barbara H. Cooks, PhD

Scripture quotations from The Authorized (King James) Version. Rights in the Authorized Version in the United Kingdom are vested in the Crown. Reproduced by permission of the Crown's patentee, Cambridge University Press

Table of Contents

Acknowledgements

To my wonderful loving husband, Rev. Andrew C. Cooks, Sr., thank you for all your support, love, understanding and patience. You are a blessing to me.

Thanks to my children Tiawian, Tyrone, Georgette, and Richelle, my son-in-law Matthew and grandson Hunter.

I am deeply blessed to have so many friends, but these two are special kinds: Angela Poltiz, Assistant Principal of Huntington High School, Shreveport, LA; and Amy Bridges, Librarian of Huntington High School, Shreveport, LA.

Special thanks also to Dr. Mark Crook, Professor of Christian Counseling, Louisiana Baptist University and Theological Seminary, Shreveport, LA.

Introduction

As Christians, we often believe our lives should be exempt from problems. We should not struggle with human emotions, and we should automatically be above certain things because we profess the name of Christ. Yes, that sounds good in theory, but it is not realistic. The truth is that even as we work day by day to become more Christ-like, it is a process. We do not get baptized one day and suddenly all our problems are washed away by the blood of Jesus. We must realize we are human and must deal with our human emotions. This realization can be a stumbling block for many Christians. Once we realize we are still dealing with anger, hurt and resentment issues, we sometimes feel the church is failing us. We are disappointed that our lives are still messed up and we are still dealing with things we thought would disappear.

I hope this book will help change the way Christians deal with life and the way we think. What I realized in this life is that we must deal with our emotions and grow to a level where we can address things honestly and ultimately come to terms with them and thus move to a greater level of understanding of who we are and have a greater commitment to God.

Dealing with forgiveness on so many levels is part of a Christian's walk. First, we must understand that we must truly accept God's forgiveness of us for our transgressions before we can forgive others. Secondly, we must forgive to grow in Christ so that our hearts will be open to love. We must even forgive the one who wronged us in very serious ways. When we are unable to forgive, it means we are stagnant in our Christian journey. Finally, forgiveness is important because it is a part of healing; when we heal, we grow. When we grow, we share the goodness of the Lord.

Chapter 1

What is Forgiveness?

To forgive means to restore a bond of love and communion when there has been a rupture. Sin ruptures our relationship with God and others, as also do offenses taken and given among people.

When the bond is broken with other people, we tend to objectify them and judge them, not seeing them as persons, but only as objects of our anger and hurt. This is our sinful reaction. We categorize people in terms of their transgression against us. The longer we nurture the anger and alienation, the more deeply the resentment takes hold in our heart, and the more it feeds on our soul. Resentment is a cancer that will destroy us if we do not forgive. This resentment leaks out and damages our relations with others when we slander and gossip about who has offended us and try to draw others to our own side. Of course, no one should want to hear such things, but we do.

Forgiveness means overlooking the sin or transgression and restoring a bond of love. It does not mean justifying the offensive action or accepting it as right, nor does it mean justifying one's own anger or sinful reaction. Forgiveness means laying aside our judgment of the other person and our own sinful reactions and accepting others for who they are.

God's forgiveness of us for our sins against Him is unconditional and absolute. God does not reject us, objectify us, or bear anger or resentment against us. These are our projections onto God of our own issues and judgment against ourselves when we sin. God does not punish us. Rather, by alienating ourselves from God, we punish ourselves and ascribe this punishment to Him. We turn in on ourselves in anger and self-hatred, and thus shatter our personhood, cutting ourselves off from His love.

By asking God for forgiveness, we open ourselves to His love and acceptance, His grace and compassion. These were there already, but we neglected them. By confessing our sins, we surrender these areas of our lives where we have justified our self-alienation from God. Repentance means not only turning away from sin, but also turning to God. Judas was remorseful for his sin but hanged himself. We need not only to be remorseful, but also to open ourselves to God.

Many people think of forgiveness as letting go or moving on. But there's more to it than that, says Bob Enright, PhD, a psychologist at the University of Wisconsin, Madison, who pioneered the study of forgiveness three decades ago. True forgiveness goes a step further, he says, offering something positive—empathy, compassion, and understanding—toward the person who hurt you. That element makes forgiveness both a virtue and a powerful construct in positive psychology.

One common but mistaken belief is that forgiveness means letting the person who hurt you off the hook. Yet forgiveness is not the same as justice, nor does it require reconciliation, Worthington explains. A former victim of abuse should not reconcile with an abuser who remains potentially dangerous, for example. But the victim can still come to a place of empathy and understanding. "Whether I forgive or don't forgive isn't going to affect whether justice is done," Worthington says.

Research has shown that forgiveness is linked to mental health outcomes such as reduced anxiety, depression and major psychiatric disorders, as well as fewer physical health symptoms and low mortality rates. In fact, researchers have amassed enough evidence of the benefits of forgiveness to fill a book: Toussaint, Worthington and David Williams, PhD, edited a 2015 book, "Forgiveness and Health," that detailed the physical and psychological benefits.

Toussaint and Worthington suggest that stress relief is probably the chief factor connecting forgiveness and well-being. We know chronic stress is bad for our health. Forgiveness allows you to let go of the chronic interpersonal stressors that cause us undue burden.

While stress relief is important, Enright believes there are other important mechanisms by which forgiveness works its magic. One of those, he suggests, is toxic anger." There's nothing wrong with a healthy anger, but when anger is very deep and long lasting, it can do a number on us systemically," he says. "When you rid yourself of anger, your muscles relax, you're less anxious, you have more energy, and your immune system can be strengthened.

Forgiveness can also help rebuild self-esteem, Enright adds. "When people are beaten down by injustice, you know who they end up not liking? Themselves. He says, "When you stand up to the pain of what happened to you and offer goodness to the person who hurt you, you change your view of yourself."

Worthington has found in his research that more forgiving types tend to have higher levels of agreeableness and lower levels of neuroticism. People who tend to ruminate are generally less quickly to forgive, since they are more likely to hold onto grudges or hurt feeling. People who have a religious faith also seem to have an upper hand in forgiving. "All of the major religions value forgiveness," Worthington notes.

Chapter 2

The Importance of Forgiveness

Forgiveness must start with acknowledging the hurt. You must choose to let go of the anger, pain, resentment and all negative feelings. It is about choosing to release yourself from the negative emotions that can ruin your life. Forgiveness comes from a Greek word that means "to release or to be relieved from an obligation or a debt." Many people who still struggle with forgiveness do so because they have not yet admitted to themselves that they are holding a worthless debt they are still trying to collect. If you are going to be healed, you must take it to God. Jesus says in Matthew 5:44 "Love your enemies." Most of us can love our friends, love those we are in good standing with, those who we get along with, but Jesus commanded us to go farther. "Love your enemies." Matthew 5:23-24 says, "Go and be reconciled to your brother" then come and offer your gift. For if you forgive men when they sin against you, your heavenly Father will also forgive you. But if you do not forgive men their sins, your Father will not forgive your sins

When Paul came to Jesus and asked, "Lord, how many times shall I forgive my brother when he sins against me" Jesus answered, "I tell you seven times, but seventy-seven times. Therefore, the kingdom of heaven is like a certain king who wanted to settle accounts with his servants. And when he began to settle accounts one brought to him who owed him ten thousand talents. But as he was not able to pay, his master commanded that he be sold, with his wife and children and all that he had, and that payment be made (Matthew 18:21-25).

Forgiveness requires that we renew our minds. Paul asks us in Romans 12:2, "Are ye transformed" by the renewing of our minds. This means we must elevate ourselves and become in true kinship with Jesus Christ. When we take on His spirit, we are consciously behaving like Him. To do so, it requires turning our lives over to Jesus and inviting Him into our hearts. Then, when the natural being, the flesh, would seek an eye for an eye, the Christian spirit seeks instead to look for other means. We die to our natural selves and allow our rebirth in Jesus to govern our very hearts. It is impossible to overcome the hard feelings when we work independently. However, when we invite Jesus into our hearts and listen for the still, small voice of the Holy Spirit, we find victory over that anger easier to gain (Kirby).

Paul also tells us that renewing our minds can help us emotionally and spiritually and to look at life in a different way. Forgiveness is a spiritual matter, but we must deal with our human emotions. We must understand that God has a plan for our lives, and we must be willing to forgive and receive His blessing through forgiveness. It is a struggle to forgive others, but you must understand this is the only option. God forgives us so that we may forgive others. When we refuse to seek His forgiveness, we are creating a barrier. We must not allow anything to separate us from God and His love. We must believe that God can do everything but fail. Mark 11:25 says, "If you are standing praying, if you hold anything against anyone, forgive them so that your Father in heaven will be able to forgive you." Jesus is a great example of forgiveness. "If our heart does not condemn us", the Bible says, "We have confidence toward God" (1 John 3:21). We cannot continue to sin in our lives and expect forgiveness. We must be free from ongoing conscious sin and rebellion against God. But if we are walking in the light, and walking in forgiveness, then the blood of Jesus Christ is continuously cleaning us from all sin (1 John 1: 7).

Forgiveness cleanses you to the point where you feel yourself cleansed of resentment and bitterness and are praying for those who have wronged you. Lack of forgiveness makes it impossible for God to forgive you. Every miracle depends 100 percent on your relationship to God the Father. That relationship is built strictly on the strength of His forgiveness of your sin.

Why Forgiveness Is Important

Forgiveness is the key. Other sins can be present, and if your heart condemns you for something else, then of course you do not have confidence before God. But it is the lack of forgiveness that most often comes between people and God.

Forgiveness is good for the heart, literally. One study from the Journal of Behavioral Medicine found forgiveness to be associated with a lower heart rate and blood pressure, as well as stress relief. Forgiveness can bring long-term health benefits for your heart and overall health. A later study shows forgiveness to be positively associated with five measures of health: physical symptoms, medications used, sleep quality, fatigue, and somatic complaints. It seems that the reduction in negative effects (depressive symptoms, strengthened spiritually, conflict management and stress relief) one finds through forgiveness all have a significant impact on overall health.

An additional study, published in the Personality and Social Psychology Bulletin, found that forgiveness restores positive thoughts, feelings, and behaviors toward the offending party. In other words, forgiveness restores the relationship to its previous positive state, but the benefits of forgiveness spill over to positive behaviors towards others outside of the relationship. Forgiveness is associated with more volunteerism, donating to charity, and other altruistic behaviors.

To sum it up, forgiveness is good for the body, your relationships, and your place in the world. This is reason enough to convince virtually anyone to do the work of letting go of anger and working on forgiveness (Scott).

Forgiveness is something all of us want to receive but most of us hesitate to give. Jesus makes it clear, however, that we cannot have it without giving it. If you forgive those who sin against you, your heavenly Father will forgive you. But if you refuse to forgive others, your Father will not forgive your sins (Matthew 6:14-15). These words allow no room for doubt or discussion. Forgiveness flows two ways. We cannot separate receiving forgiveness from extending forgiveness. Forgiveness is at the core of emotional well-being. It is fair to say that unforgiving people are emotionally sick. Their bitterness is a disease of the spirit, and it is inevitable that the unforgiving person eventually will experience physical illness as well. Anger causes surges of adrenaline and secretes other powerful chemicals that attack the body. The stress we carry when we refuse to give or receive forgiveness affects our hearts, minds, and bodies. To make matters worse, both rage and depression contribute to obsessive behaviors such as overeating, being a workaholic, overspending, and even addictions to pornography and mood-altering drugs. We cannot rid ourselves of emotional pain and its side effects unless we are willing to forgive. Unresolved anger keeps us from moving forward because it locks us in a time machine, frozen on the exact moment when an offense occurred. Fear of further injury makes us unwilling to move to new levels of relationship, not only with those who have hurt us but with anyone who represents a similar threat (Karremans).

Forgiveness is never easy, but it can be done more easily with a few exercises and the right mindset. First, keep in mind that forgiveness is something you do for yourself to sever your emotional attachment to what happened. (Think of letting your hand off a hot burner on the stove, it remains hot, but you're moving yourself away from it for your own safety.) Also, remind yourself that you are moving forward, and forgiving this person lets them (or at least what they have done) stay in the past as you move on. Journaling, prayer, or meditation, and loving kindness can all be helpful in easing yourself into forgiveness as well (Worthington).

Forgiveness cannot begin until we admit our own failures. If we cannot do that much, we can neither give nor receive forgiveness. We cannot receive forgiveness without acknowledging our need for it, and we cannot extend forgiveness without admitting that because of our own imperfect condition we have no right to withhold forgiveness from anyone else. For Christians, forgiveness is nonnegotiable; it is the very essence of our faith (North).

We should be clear on this. A healthy Christian is one who puts aside malicious traits of an evil sinful nature and embraces others in love. What comes out of love is the release of our feelings of betrayal and hurt.

The Christian is called to model kindness, love, empathy, and compassion, and out of this forgiveness will flow. God wants us to get with it, to wake up, and seize the wonders and opportunities He gives us. An unforgiving attitude, and its ugly rotten fruits, will choke us off from His wonders (Krejcir).

Ephesians 4:29-32 tells us, " not to let unwholesome talk come out of your mouths, but only what is helpful for building others up according to their needs, that it may benefit those who listen. And do not grieve the Holy Spirit of God, with whom you were sealed for the day of redemption. Get rid of all bitterness, rage and anger, brawling and slander, along with every form of malice. Be kind and compassionate to one another, forgiving each other, just as in Christ God forgave you" (KJV).

John 13:34 tells us, "a new command I give you: Love one another. As I have loved you, so you must love one another. By this all men will know that you are my disciples, if you love one another" (NIV).

Forgiveness is hard. Isaiah tells us, "For my thoughts are not your thoughts, neither are your ways my ways,' declares the Lord. 'As the heavens are higher than the earth, so are my ways higher than your ways and my thoughts than your thoughts'" (Isaiah 55:8-9, NIV).

True forgiveness is one of the hardest things to accomplish in the human experience, even for mature

Christians. Yet, this is our mandate, and call. Forgiveness is hard because it demands a surrender of our right to get even. Forgiveness even causes suffering for the person who was wronged, the victim. The suffering, from our human perspective and reasoning, should belong to the instigator of the wrong. It is natural to consider this unfair. And yes, it is unfair; it was unfair for our Lord to go through what He did to forgive us (Enright).

Forgiveness is hard, also, because we can easily avoid it; we can walk the other way and execute revenge. It would be considered justified in the eyes of our friends, our relatives, and especially of society. We could even receive a medal for coming up with a good scheme for revenge.

Forgiveness is complete. Colossians tells us, "Therefore, as God's chosen people, holy and dearly loved, clothe yourselves with compassion, kindness, humility, gentleness and patience. Bear with each other and forgive whatever grievances you may have against one another. Forgive as the Lord forgave you. And over all these virtues put on love, which binds them all together in perfect unity" (Colossians 3: 12-14, NIV).

Forgiveness is so rare in our society. For it to become a powerful witnessing tool, it must be complete. Forgiveness does not make light of the wrong, nor should it give a license to others to take advantage of us, but they may. Yet, it is well worth it. Out of the completeness of forgiveness will come the forgetting. Then, out of the forgetting, will come the healing. The healing we get from forgiveness will close the wounds we receive; it will allow us to go on with life. It will prevent our suffering and setbacks from becoming our identity and obsession. For without forgiveness, we give in to the bitterness that will consume and take us over, that it may give us a purpose for existing, but not for living. If we just try to forget, and then agonize over it, we will get nowhere; but through the process of surrender (Galatians 2; 20-21) will come the forgetting. Forgetting is a process, and we can't expect it to come right away (Krejcir).

Forgiveness is costly, Luke tells us, "but I tell you who hear me: Love your enemies, do good to those who hate you, bless those who curse you, pray for those who mistreat you. If someone strikes you on one cheek, turn to him the other also. If someone takes your cloak, do not stop him from taking your tunic. Give to everyone who asks you, and if anyone takes what belongs to you, do not demand it back. Do to others as you would have them do to you" (Luke 6:27-31, NIV).

When we forgive, it may incur a cost to us. We should realize, and even welcome, that cost. These go against our inclination and will, but remember, the vengeance belongs to the Lord. We are to never forget the cost our Lord paid on our behalf. No cost we could ever incur could compare with the cost He paid for us. When we forgive, we will be refocusing our plans for our pain into God's plan, and God's ways. So, our pain is relieved, and our life can go on in a better direction (Krejcir).

We can live an improved quality of life when we forgive. Our relationships can grow, and we can become more useful to others, and especially, to God. When we understand that it does involve cost, we can gain the right mindset for forgiveness. We will realize from Scripture not to base it on feelings and desires but focus on what forgiveness really is. We can see it as what Christ gave us, as He was our example. John 3:16 is the example of what forgiveness cost our Lord. His undeserved, painful death and separation from the Father was a substitution for what we deserved. This was our Lord's suffering and cost. In comparison, the cost for us will be very minimal and limited, and we need to keep this in view, using it as our strength to get through it (Marrazzo).

Our cost is to live with the consequence of the evil that was brought on us. We then take the responsibility for the hurt brought on to us. Understanding this is hard, even for the mature Christian, and virtually impossible for the non-Christian since it goes against the common sense of society. In the eyes of the world, the suffering should be put upon the one who did the wrong. Yet, the Scriptural view is a beacon, a witness to the supremacy of Christ (Wright).

We normally avoid this form of suffering, but we are called to face it. We need to accept the consequences of the wrong, such as a parent forgiving a child for breaking a priceless object. The parent bears the cost to either replace it, or suffers without it, and the child gets off free (well, with some sort of punishment). This is the cost of suffering. Forgiveness chooses to suffer. It is very hard to make that voluntary choice to take on the suffering, even when we do not deserve it; yet, we must do it to grow in our walk with our Lord, and to grow toward our full potential (Weir).

Humanity owes a great deal to the Creator of the universe, and our willful disobedience to our Creator is a slap in His face. We owe a debt we could never conceive or repay. Yet, most people live their lives as an insult to what Christ has done. Christ still pursues them with the ultimate love. Christ did not owe our debt, yet He paid it.

The relation between what Christ went through so that we could be forgiven, and the call for us to take on the responsibility for a sin we did not commit, will give us a deeper understanding into the character and nature of God. From this, we should mature to a deeper level, and be used in a greater way to further the cause of Christ. Therefore, the cost accepted by our Lord is the greatest cost of all. We need to realize this and respond accordingly to one another (Scott).

Forgiveness is worth the agony we may go through, because it will heal the wounds and relieve the pain. This will help us to redirect our wrong path onto the right direction. Be the person who forgives. Do not be the person who refuses to.

Why Forgiveness Is Important

Forgiveness is defined as a conscious, deliberate decision to release feelings of resentment or vengeance toward a person or group who has harmed you, regardless of whether you believe they deserve your forgiveness. Remember the act of forgiving is for you the forgiver, not the person you are forgiving.

Forgiveness does not mean that you gloss over or deny the seriousness of an offense against you. It does not mean forgetting or excusing what has been done. It does not mean you have to reconcile with the person or release them from legal accountability. Lamott says forgiveness is for the forgiver. It brings the forgiver peace and hopefully freedom from anger.

Jack Kornfield defines forgiveness as having the capacity to let go, to release the suffering, the sorrows, the burdens of the pains and betrayals of the past, and instead to choose the mystery of love. Forgiveness shifts us from a small separate sense of ourselves to a capacity to renew, to let go, to live in love.

The Mayo Clinic explains that letting go of grudges and bitterness can make way for happiness, health and peace. Forgiveness can lead to healthier relationships, greater spiritual and psychological well-being, less anxiety, stress and hostility, lower blood pressure, fewer symptoms of depression, stronger immune system, improved heart health and higher self-esteem.

Fred Luskin is one of the pioneers in the science and practice of forgiveness. He offers us nine steps toward forgiveness:

1. Understand how you feel about what happened and be able to explain why the situation is not okay. Then discuss it with someone you trust.

2. Commit to yourself to feel better; remember forgiveness is for you and no one else.

3. Remember forgiveness doesn't mean you have to reconcile with the person who upset you; it does not condone the action. In forgiveness you are seeking peace for yourself.

4. Recognize that the distress now is coming from the hurt feeling and physical upset you are currently suffering, not from what offended you or hurt you when it happened.

5. Once you feel upset, practice stress management to soothe your body's fight to flight response. Take a deep breath.

6. Stop expecting things from other people that they do not choose to give up.

7. Put your energy into looking for another way to get your positive goals met other

than through the experience that has hurt
you.

8. Remember that living well is the best
    revenge. Instead of focusing on your
    wounded feelings, and thereby giving power
    over you to the person who caused you pain,
    look for the love, beauty, and kindness
    around you. Put more energy into
    appreciating what you have rather than
    attending to what you do not have.

9. Amend the way you look at your past, so
    you remind yourself of your heroic choice to
    forgive.

        Remember letting go of the anger
and practicing forgiveness is for your own
peace of mind.

Chapter 3

The Challenges of Forgiveness

Forgiveness can be difficult when the person who wronged us does not seem to deserve our forgiveness. It feels like we are letting them "off the hook" when they are the one who wronged us. It is hard to remember that forgiveness benefits the forgiver more than the one who is forgiven.

Ultimately, forgiveness is especially challenging because it is hard to let go of what has happened. It can be difficult to accept some things in life and forgiving someone who has committed unacceptable behaviors can be difficult when we are having trouble letting go of anger about the events and accepting what happened to us (Scott). Forgiveness is a choice we make when we decide it is more important to be happy than to be right. We chose to forgive when we decide we are ready to let ourselves be free. When we hang on to resentments we cannot escape them. We may escape the people who triggered the resentments, but unfortunately the feelings we are running from will make their way back into other relationships.

"When forgiveness is impossible in their own strength, may they be willing to receive your strength to forgive, for through Christ they have strength for anything" (Philippians 4:13).

Help them see that forgiveness is not an emotion. They don't have to feel like forgiving, but they choose to act as a matter of will, made possible by the power of the Spirit who lives within them (Ephesians 3:16). Forgiveness is something all of us want, but very few of us are willing to give. All of us want others to forgive us; we want people to be understanding when it comes to our faults and our failures. However, when it comes to us forgiving others, we are reluctant. We are hesitant. Jesus makes it clear in His Word that forgiveness is something you cannot have unless you are willing to give it. Forgiveness must be a two-way street. You must be willing to give it, to receive it.

The Bible says we cannot rid ourselves of emotional pain and side effects unless we are willing to forgive. Unresolved anger keeps us from moving forward because it locks us in time machines and freezes us on the exact wrong someone has done to us. Anger causes us to be fearful of any future injuries and makes us unwilling to move ahead and go to another level in a relationship. It damages our ability to bond, not just with those who have hurt us, but with others who we see as threats and the cause of our experiences (Kirby).

Forgiveness can occur according to God's will. People choose to forgive out of trust. Forgiveness often takes a longer time than expected and, in some cases, requires a lifetime decision for it to be possible. Prayer is one of the ways to give forgiveness. Forgiveness should be done willingly and with respect. Forgiveness can sometimes feel impossible or even undesirable. Other times, we forgive only to be hurt again and conclude that forgiving was foolish. Both situations arise from confusion about what forgiveness really means. Forgiveness does not require that we forget or condone another's actions, or the harm caused. In fact, for self-protection rather than anger, we may decide to never see the person again. Forgiveness does not mean to justify or play down the hurt caused. Often, codependents forgive and forget, and continue to put themselves in harm's way. They forgive and then rationalize or minimize their loved one's abuse or addiction. This is their denial. They may even contribute to it by enabling (Lancer).

Researchers are trying to determine the ways in which the spiritual act of forgiveness can promote personal, inter-relational, and social well-being. Harnden is enthusiastic about the personal benefits of forgiveness. "It not only heightens the potential for reconciliation," he says, "but also releases the offender from prolonged anger, rage, and stress that have been linked to physiological problems, such as cardiovascular diseases, high blood pressure, hypertension, cancer, and other psychosomatic illness" (Enright).

Robert Enright, professor of educational psychology at University of Wisconsin-Madison and president of the International Forgiveness Institute is at the forefront of interpersonal forgiveness research. Together with philosopher Joanna North, Enright writes about the benefits of forgiveness to society. "It is an obvious fact that we live in a world where violence, hatred, and animosity surround us on all sides. We hear much about the social causes of crime, poverty, unemployment, and illiteracy, for example. We sometimes hear about the need for tolerance and cooperation, compassion, and understanding." However, almost never do we hear public leaders declaring their belief that forgiveness can bring people together, heal their wounds, and alleviate the bitterness and resentment caused by wrongdoing. Enright and North believe that forgiveness might be useful in helping those who have been affected by cruelty, crime, and violence, and might play a valuable role in reconciling warring parties and restoring harmony between people.

In recent studies conducted on forgiveness coping strategies, it was found that men respond positively when it was presented as a challenge to them, and negatively when it involved emotion-focused coping. For women, however, it was found to be positively associated with emotion-focused coping and acceptance, and negatively associated with avoidance. Thus, based on this finding, if you are a man, it is more helpful to approach forgiveness as a challenge, or goal to accomplish. If you are a woman working on acceptance, then understanding, and compassion may lead you there more successfully (Hereford).

Remember first that the act of forgiving is more for your own benefit than anyone else's. Secondly, forgiveness takes time, so be patient with you. Certainly, it can be difficult to separate what you feel emotionally with what make sense to do logically. However, if you commit to putting your energies on focusing on the benefits of forgiveness, you can more easily move forward with your life.

Forgiveness and Reconciliation: What they are and what they aren't:

There has been much misunderstanding about forgiveness and its companion, reconciliation. Dr. E. Dowd describes the benefits and pitfalls of forgiveness and tries to dispel some misconceptions about it.

Forgiveness can be both intra-personal (an attitude change) and interpersonal (a change in relations between people). In genuine forgiveness, one who has suffered an injury chooses to abandon rights to resentment and retaliation and instead offers mercy and understanding. It is voluntary and unconditional and does not depend on the offender's response, although the offender's response may help.

What forgiveness is not:

1. It is not pardoning (sparing legal penalties), condoning (which implies a justified offense), excusing (implying the offender has a defensible reason) or forgetting (denying existence of injury).

2. It is not necessarily reconciliation. This implies continuation or reestablishment of a previous relationship and is based on the trustworthiness of the offender. Sometimes the offender is not even present, as in death.

3. Forgiveness does not necessarily demonstrate the moral superiority of the injured party.

What do people do when they forgive?

1. They feel empathy for the transgressor, trying to understand the reasons behind the injury.

2. They have more generous feelings about the transgressor.

3. They stop ruminating about the transgression. The more people ruminate about an offense, the more difficulty they have forgiving the offense.

Dimensions of Forgiveness

Dr. Dowd (2017) says forgiveness involves both internal and interpersonal activities. The former changes cognitive appraisals and interpretations such as anger and hostility; the latter changes the relationship with the offender and implies no further revenge or reparations. But the fear often is that the offender may then not have to feel as guilty or change future behavior.

There are several types of forgiveness:

1. Hollow forgiveness. The injured party expresses forgiveness but does not really feel it. He/she may continue to harbor resentments, but the perpetrator may feel the matter is over and "back to normal." But expressing forgiveness may be the first step to making the commitment to forgive, because changed behavior really can change

attitudes. Hollow forgiveness is better than nothing.

2. Silent forgiveness. The injured party changes his/her attitude but does not express it. This allows the perpetrator to continue to feel guilty but reduces the negative feelings of the injured party. It seems manipulative but has several advantages. First, it has many of the advantages of forgiveness (reduction of negative feelings) without the disadvantages (loss of the perpetrator's concessions and restitutions). Second, it may provide safety in certain situations, e.g. with an abusive spouse. Third, it may work well in exchange relationships where we need resources from other people. You can use the "after all I've sacrificed for you…" model.

3. Total forgiveness. The injured party ceases to feel resentful or upset about the offense and the perpetrator is released from further obligation and guilt. There may indeed be a total reconciliation here.

4. No forgiveness ("total grudge"). Nothing but hate. Everyone is taught to hate and hold a grudge against the perpetrator.

There are several advantages of forgiveness:

1. A continuation of negative emotions may undermine one's mental (and even physical) health. Anger can, in the short run, feel empowering but it doesn't last. If you have a disposition to forgive, it may reduce your interpersonal hostility in general.

2. It can restore needed close and caring relationships; a lack of forgiveness tends to undermine all relationships and can lead to having few friends or intimates. It promotes relationship harmony.

3. A refusal to forgive invariably hurts the injured party more than the offender. A famous Rabbi once said that a refusal to forgive if forgiveness is genuinely asked for is as great as the original offense. The victim role is associated with misfortune and passivity and identifying with it can undermine one's ability to function.

4. Forgiving is transformational rather than conservational. It changes one's motivation from self-protection to self-enhancement. It changes one's goal from avoiding pain to pursuing peace—peace of mind and peace with others. It is empowering because it eliminates the

victim role which is disempowering. It encourages empathy. But dropping our self-protective stance is difficult indeed for all of us.

Disadvantages of forgiveness (advantages of holding grudges):

1. Forgiveness involves relinquishing future claims for restitution: in other words, the offender no longer owes anything. In economic terms, it reduces the injured party's future resources. There are tangible and material benefits to be gained by holding grudges.

2. Not forgiving helps one to retain a sense of moral superiority (righteous indignation); forgiving renounces it. But in many religions, forgiving itself has been viewed as morally commendable.

3. Forgiving may increase the possibility that the transgression will recur; not forgiving may result in greater power in the victim that may reduce the chances of reoccurrence. Not forgiving means the injured party can continually remind the perpetrator of the offense. In that sense,

not forgiving can feel empowering because forgiveness reduces one's options.

4. Forgiving can be risky if the perpetrator denies wrongdoing. Forgiveness may remove the last obstacle to a repeat. An apology involves the implicit assumption that the transgression will not be repeated. One study showed that the perpetrator's response was the best predictor of forgiveness and an apology correlated with high forgiveness. Apologies also helped people feel more empathic towards perpetrators.

5. Transgressions may hurt the injured party's pride or self-esteem and forgiving may feel like accepting a loss of face or self-esteem. This may account for "silent forgiveness," which avoids a public loss of face. Forgiveness may be misinterpreted as weakness.

6. Forgiveness means relinquishing a claim on revenge. Revenge can be a positive, empowering feeling at least in the short run.

7. Non-forgiveness may arise from principles or moral standards; forgiving may feel like condoning immorality. Strong adherence

to standards of justice may imply that some acts should not be forgiven.

Forgiveness can be considered both a trait and a state. The difference between the two being the prevalence of forgiveness for an individual over time, whilst the state of forgiveness may be short term or apply to one situation. Those who possess the trait of forgiveness will have a blanket approach towards stressful or painful situations where forgiveness is more easily achieved.

A study conducted in Taiwan by Wang (2008) researched the relationship between the big five personality traits and the tendency to forgive. The research found that those people who were agreeable and emotionally stable found it easier to forgive. This evidence shows that through emotional stability and higher agreeableness you are likely to forgive those who wronged you.

Forgiveness is a key part of many religious and civil codes (e.g. Restorative Justice) because it helps societies to heal and function. Numerous studies have found that the positive effects of forgiveness are for those who forgive rather than those who are forgiven. One such study found that those who forgave had less anger, less stress, less rumination and lowered reactivity in comparison to those who held onto their anger and pain (Harris et al., 2001).

Chapter 4

Biblical View of Forgiveness

Forgiveness exists as an essential and inescapable aspect of Christian life. Jesus Himself gave us the supreme example of forgiveness in the face of the most ignoble cruelty inflicted upon Him on the cross: "Father, forgive them," he prayed, "for they do not know what they do" (Luke 23:34). The Scripture challenges us to follow His example: "bearing with one another and forgiving one another. If anyone has a complaint against another; even as Christ forgave you, so you also must do" (Col. 3:13).

Indeed, Jesus places forgiveness as central to the Christian way of life and puts it in the center of the prayer that He taught His disciples to pray, a prayer that Christians have prayed for two millennia. That prayer links God's forgiveness of sins to our willingness to forgive others (Matt. 6-12). "And whenever you stand praying, if you have anything against anyone, forgive him that your Father in heaven may also forgive your trespasses. But if you do not forgive, neither will your Father in heaven forgive your trespasses "(Mark 11:25).

Matthew defines forgiveness as canceling the offender's "debt" toward us. Not only do we cancel indebtedness or obligation toward us, we also renounce any claim or liability against the forgiven person. Viewed thus, forgiveness becomes intensely personal, and relates more to the forgiver than to the forgiven. Forgiveness is no mere form but must spring from the heart. Even if one cannot forget the incident in an absolute sense, no room for any grudge or resentment should live in the forgiving person's mind. Such an experience may be difficult in human terms, indeed impossible for human strength; it calls upon us to claim that great promise, "with God all things are possible" (Matt. 19:26).

Forgiveness is a blessing for our own benefit and salvation; we are called to forgive. We must let go of anger, resentment, hurt, hatred, bitterness, desire for revenge, and getting even. Instead, we must move on with God. Sin, as a two-edged sword, damages the victim and damages the sinner. Likewise, with forgiveness: refusal to forgive damages the victim as they cling to their pain, anger, and hurt, and fail to move on with a life of peace that comes from the experience of having forgiven, for a refusal to accept forgiveness leaves one in sin. Spiritually, the only real healing for a victim is to forgive.

How often should we forgive? Peter came to the Lord and asked, "How many times shall I forgive my brother when he sins against me?" Jesus answered, "I tell you, not seven times but seventy-seven times" (Matthew 18:21). Luke 6:37 says, "Do not judge and you will not be judged; Do not condemn, and you will not be condemned; Forgive, and you will be forgiven."

Jackson's (2017) study looks at a biblical portrayal of forgiveness from two vantage points: divine forgiveness, i.e. that which proceeds from God to man; and human forgiveness, that which we extend to one another.

Greek New Testament defines "forgive," in two terms. The first term is aphesis, literally meaning "to send away." The word had a variety of meaning in secular Greek, but in its thirty-six times in the New Testament, it is always associated with the "pardon of sins" (Krejcir1994, 242).

The second term used for "forgiveness" is charizomai, which signifies "to bestow a favor or "to "show kindness." In Romans 8:32, charizomai is rendered "shall freely give." In his second Corinthian epistle, Paul admonishes the saints to forgive a certain wayward brother (presumably the offender mentioned in 1 Corinthians 5), that he might not be overcome with sorrow (2 Corinthians 2:7). In Colossians 3:13, Paul twice uses the term—once for the forgiveness we ought to extend to one another, and then to that which we received from Christ. There is the suggestion that just as the Lord graciously forgave us, we should wholeheartedly extend the same kindness to others. Although, as we shall presently note, forgiveness is not extended unconditionally.

There are numerous exciting expressions of figurative language in the Scriptures that portray a rich picture of forgiveness flowing from the mind of God. David praised the Creator for his loving kindness because, "As far as the east is from the west, so far hath he removed our transgressions from us" (Psalm 103:12). The good king Hezekiah thanked the Lord for his redemption, proclaiming that "you have thrown all my sins behind your back" (Isaiah 38:17). The prophet Micah is even more picturesque. He describes Jehovah as treading our iniquities under his feet, and then casting the residue into the sea (7:19 KJV).

When one turns to God in obedience, his sins are "blotted out" (Acts 3:19; cf. Psalm 51:1, 9). The Greeks used this term of "washing out" the ink from a papyrus sheet so that it might be used for writing again (Moulton 1963, 221).

The Scriptures use the term "redemption" as an equivalent for "forgiveness." Paul declared that it is "in Christ that we have our "redemption (apolutrosis) through his blood, the forgiveness of our trespasses" (Ephesians 1:7). Redemption originally had to do with buying back a slave from his captivity (Arndt and Gingrich 1967, 95); in the New Testament it suggests the offer of freedom from the consequences of sin based on Jesus' atoning death (cf. Romans 3:24). The Lord was an umblemished sacrifice that bore the penalty for our sins (Isaiah 53:5-6).

Jackson suggests that the idea of forgiveness stirs the soul and has some intriguing implications. First, "forgiveness" implies an offense. If there is no breach of propriety, no forgiveness is needed. The fact that an accountable human requires forgiveness, therefore, suggests that they committed offenses (sins) against their Creator. This suggests that a standard of conduct that has been violated. The Bible addresses both matters in one verse; an inspired apostle declares that sins are "lawlessness" (1John 3:4). "Lawlessness" literally means "without law," and it represents a "revolt against God" (Bromiley 1985, 654). All of us, to a degree, are outlaws!

Second, forgiveness implies a personal inability to remedy the violation of law. In one of his parables, Jesus told of a man who was head-over-heels in debt to his lord. In describing the hapless condition of the debtor, the Lord said that "he had not wherewith to pay" (Matthew 18:25). That man represents each of us. We do not have the wherewithal to remedy our despicable condition. One cannot un-tell a lie once it is told; he cannot un-commit adultery after the foul deed has been done. Sin cannot be undone by any human maneuver. And so, according to the language of the parable, the Lord (representing God) "being moved with compassion, released him (the debtor), and forgave him the debt" (18-27).

Among psychologists, forgiveness and reconciliation are typically viewed as separate constructs. This distinction is often adaptive, making it possible for a person to forgive his offender or to forget the offense without returning into a dangerous relationship. But to what extent does this privatized and secularized view of forgiveness conflict with the religious construct of forgiveness that many clients and their religious leaders may hold? Two survey studies are reported here. The first assessed the opinions of academic psychologists and Christian theologians regarding the distinction between forgiveness and reconciliation. The second survey assessed the opinions of expert psychologists and Christian theologians who have published books on the topic of forgiveness. Both quantitative and qualitative analyses revealed that psychologists are more inclined to distinguish between forgiveness and reconciliation than Christian theologians (Frise, McCann).

Forgiveness is a decision to release or let go of your right to punish another and choosing through the power of God's love to hold onto the other rather than his or her offense. In this process of forgiving, the first barrier you should remove is within yourself.

Forgiving is not the same as forgetting. It is not a divine form of amnesia. God does not ask us to live as people without a history or pretend that sins never happened. In fact, being able to recall how God has delivered us through marital storms, empowering us to confess, forgive, and overcome, can give us hope and an anchor in future storms. Stories of forgiveness and reconciliation can also become part of the way you seek to strengthen and encourage others in their marriages. Remember that it is one thing to dwell on an incident with thankfulness for how God has worked in your life but quite another to dwell on it and find your anger and hurt reawakened (Smith).

Forgiveness is a sacrifice in the sense that you are choosing the more difficult path. You are sacrificing the temporary comfort of ignoring the problem or the temporary pleasure of erecting a wall of bitterness and instead doing the hard and sometimes painful work of moving toward the one who has wounded you.

Nothing matches the spiritual freedom that forgiveness brings to the soul. In fact, it captures God's attention because it extends His mercy. It frees one's bondage of self and purifies.

The most compelling evidence of the Holy Spirit's existence is one's ability to let go of wrongdoings from others. This act of holiness shows the inner changes Christ makes to a believer's spirit. As a result, from forgiveness, the believer's bond with God strengthens and a spiritual love for others increases.

Forgiving others takes courage beyond the flesh. The strength needed to achieve this Christian action must come from Christ. And once a person is in the power of Jesus, the most troublesome wrongs caused by others become forgivable. When we forgive others it frees the mind, heart, and soul from transgression. This separation from sin is not by accident but a result of Christ's love. It is important to realize Jesus is God's way and freedom from a hardened heart comes from a life centered in Christ.

When you are unwilling to forgive, your mind becomes entangled with sinful thoughts. You are unable to find peace of mind because pride controls your thoughts on the person who wronged you. This causes problems because it takes you away from Christ and leaves you in the midst of sin. Another trouble with not forgiving is the effect it has on your heart. Here it stirs up resentments leading to bitterness and cuts you off from God's mercy. This spiritual turmoil is a stumbling block placing you at odds with Christ. The longer we hold onto this wrongfulness, the more distant we become from God's light (Trujillo).

Understanding the God of Grace

In Scripture, "grace" draws together several key biblical concepts. In the Old Testament, it is the "favor" of God, (hen in Hebrew); it is being merciful and compassionate (hanan); it is steadfast love (hesed). In the New Testament the Greek word charis builds upon these concepts to communicate the favor of God understood, particularly, through the lens of the forgiveness and redemption we find in Jesus' death and resurrection.

But understanding grace is about more than dissecting biblical terms; it understands we gain as we grow in intimacy with our God of grace. When God revealed himself to Moses, God described himself this way: "Yahweh! The Lord! The God of compassion and mercy! I am slow to anger and filled with unfailing love and faithfulness. I lavish unfailing love to a thousand generations. I forgive iniquity, rebellion, and sin" (Exodus 34:6-7). God is just, righteous and holy—but grace is also central to his character. It's in God's DNA at the very core of God's being. As we journey through life with this God of compassion, mercy, unfailing love, and forgiveness, we experience his grace…and it changes us.

Scripture tells us that through grace we are forgiven. God in the Bible used people to show his grace in the story of Hosea and Gomer. Hosea married a prostitute, at the request of God. But he was still faithful to her. Their marriage symbolizes God's faithfulness to unfaithful Israel… and it also depicts us, does it not? It hurts to be honest and see ourselves in Gomer. But this illustrates the extent of God's forgiving love for us (Trujillo).

First, we must understand that forgiveness does not mean that the sins are to be ignored. There are moral and civil consequences for our actions. But we must remember that God wants us to have compassion and a forgiving spirit that is God-like (cf. Matthew 18:27), as difficult as that may be to achieve. We must reflect upon our own past and be painfully aware of how we have disappointed the Lord so terribly and frequently. We tend to minimize our own blunders and yet maximize the mistakes of others. It is a rather terrible thing when we forget the many sins of which we have been forgiven (2 Peter 1:9). We must learn to forgive because to do otherwise is most harmful to our own state of mind and even physical well-being. Bitterness and an unforgiving spirit can bring much stress and distress to both mind and body. Forgiving can be a matter of life and death. We must try to master the art of forgiving for our own sake and the sake of others.

Chapter 5

The Science of Forgiveness

During the past decade, there has been more and
more research into forgiveness. Whereas previously the
discussion of forgiveness was left to the religious, it is
now gaining attention as an academic discipline studied
not only by philosophers and theologians, but also by
psychologists and physicians. Even neuroscientists are
studying the biology of forgiveness and exploring
evolutionary barriers in the brain that hinder the act of
forgiving. Some are even looking to see if there might
be a forgiveness gene somewhere in our DNA. As
modern forgiveness research evolves, the findings
clearly show that forgiving transforms people mentally,
emotionally, spiritually, and even physically. In
*Forgive for Good: A Proven Prescription for Health
and Happiness*, psychologist Fred Luskin writes, "In

careful scientific studies, forgiveness training has been shown to reduce depression, increase hopefulness, decrease anger, improve spiritual connection, and increase emotional self-confidence. "Research also shows that people who are more forgiving report fewer health and mental problems, and fewer physical symptoms of stress.

As more and more scientists document the healing power of forgiveness, they also look at the mentally and physically corrosive effects of not forgiving. Hanging on to anger and resentment and living in a constant state of stress can damage the heart as well as the soul. In fact, research has shown that failure to forgive may be a risk factor for heart disease, high blood pressure, and a score of other chronic stress-related illnesses. Medical and psychological studies have also shown that a person holding on to anger and resentment is at an increased risk for anxiety, depression, and insomnia, and more likely to suffer from high blood pressure, ulcers, migraines, heart attacks, and even cancer. The reverse is also true. Genuine forgiveness can transform these ailments. Forgiveness is good for you; science is just confirming what people have known for millennia. Health benefits are only the beginning. To forgive is also to release oneself from whatever trauma and hardship you have experienced and reclaim your life as your own.

Katheryn R. Meek (2001) said the concept of forgiveness no longer falls solely under the umbrella of religious thought. Social scientists are beginning to recognize the powerful practical and therapeutic benefits that forgiveness offers in a broken and isolated world. She says forgiveness is a concept deeply rooted within a faith context. Indeed, in the Bible forgiveness is the most crucial concept, the basis for relational healing both horizontally (within community) and vertically (with God). Historically, the study of forgiveness fell under the purview of pastors and other religious leaders who have long known the powerful healing benefits that come with both giving and receiving forgiveness. Lives are transformed as hope takes the place of guilt, anger, loneliness, and fear, as relationships are restored, and the love of God transforms a life.

However, all who struggle to grant forgiveness in the face of grave injustices recognize that forgiving is difficult. Yet, religious leaders have consistently maintained that forgiveness is both required and provides the foundation for a new community of hope.

In 1980 a group of social scientists, with varying faith commitments, sought to understand and implement the power of forgiveness in society at large. The Campaign for Forgiveness Research cites recent studies showing that the practice of forgiveness is directly related to emotional healing and the building of peaceful ranging and can be seen in various personal and social contexts: among Vietnam veterans coping with post-traumatic stress disorders; among victims of sexual abuse and domestic violence; among HIV/AIDS patients; and among the diverse clusters of people facing end of life issues. Given the link between health and forgiveness, is it any wonder that many people now think forgiveness can reduce the severity of heart diseases, prolong the life of cancer patients, and reduce levels of crime (by quenching the desire for revenge)?

In 1985 at the University of Madison, Roy Lloyd and Robert Enright began a journey of investigating the scientific outcomes when people forgive. They first looked at the definition of forgiveness. They found a common theme from the ancient literature across Hebrew, Confucian, Buddhist, Christian, Muslim, and Hindu writings. Forgiveness, from modern philosophical writing, has the same underlying theme. When unjustly treated by others, a person forgives when she struggles to abandon resentment and to offer beneficence toward the unjust person or people.

Forgiveness is a part of mercy, and so it can appear to come from a position of weakness as the unjustly treated person offers the olive branch. Forgiveness is anything but weakness, because the forgiver is not condoning, excusing, forgetting, or necessarily even reconciling with the other because none of these qualities is a mortal virtue centered in goodness as is forgiveness. When a person forgives, he does not abandon justice, but instead exercises this virtue along with the mercy that is forgiveness.

Lloyd and Enright devised a pathway that in theory should help people after their scientific journey.

They studied people who were willing to forgive. That pathway is now described in the book *"Forgiveness Is a Choice"* published by the American Psychological Association. The book outlines twenty "guideposts" or steps in the forgiveness process. The short version of that process is as follows:

First, the one who forgives examines the degree to which the injustice has affected her emotions, such as anger, hatred, resentment and so forth. Feeling rotten inside is a great motivator to change.

Second, if a person decides to change his inner world, which was affected by the other's injustice, he then decides to practice forgiveness, understanding that he is offering merciful goodness and not condoning.

Next comes what the late Lewis Smedes called "seeing with new eyes," as the forgiver sees that the injuring person is more than the offenses she has committed. The forgiver sees the unconditional worth of the other as a person, which can lead to empathy and compassion and eventually to the willingness to offer goodness to the other out of mercy. It is here that forgiveness takes root, opening the possibility of restored emotional and relational health.

Lloyd and Enright decided to put the pathway of forgiveness to test through randomized clinical trials. Among the groups they studied were emotionally abused women, college students hurt by emotionally distant parents, the elderly hurt by family members, incest survivors, and people recovering in a drug rehabilitation facility, men who were angry and who had cardiac problems, and hospice patients who wanted to tie up the loose ends of family estrangement before passing on. In each study, they found that people willingly walked the path of forgiveness by offering the gift of mercy to the unjust. Those in the forgiveness group experienced emotional health improvement compared to those in the control groups. The incest study showed positive results including the elimination of psychological depression, which remained low even one year after the forgiveness program ended. Science tells us that forgiveness bolsters emotional health and provides a way of healing for those treated unjustly.

After studying how forgiveness improved the psychological health of the adult populations, Lloyd and Enright wanted to see how children could benefit. In 2002, they developed a forgiveness education curriculum for children in war torn, impoverished, and oppressed areas of the globe to help them learn about forgiveness and to practice it in a small way in school and in the family, if they chose to do so. All instruction was delivered by the classroom teacher, to preserve cultural nuances. All lessons were delivered through the medium of story, such as Dr. Seuss' *Horton Hears a Who*, or Disney's *The Fox and the Hound*. As the children see the story characters making their way out of difficulty via both justice and forgiveness, they are given insight into these virtues and how they can be worked out in small and large groups. Among the groups' studies it was shown that the levels of anger decreased. It was their hope that such anger reduction, if it continued, might help them to see, when they are adults, the best paths toward justice.

The hope was that forgiveness education would catch on worldwide. Areas such as Rwanda, Nigeria, Korea, and Iran have requested materials from educators and psychologists on forgiveness education, hoping to educate their people and bring peace to the world.

Chapter 6

Forgiving Others—The Divine Example

We have a divine example for forgiving others. God knew that man needed forgiveness, so He sent His son Jesus to deliver all of humankind from the eternal consequences of sin (1 John 4:9-10). Colossians 3:13 says, "Bear with each other and forgive whatever grievances you may have against one another, Forgive as the Lord forgave you." Jesus not only had the power to forgive, but to grant us the ability to forgive others just as we have been forgiven.

If you reach out to God and seek a deeper relationship with Him, He will draw near to you, and you will find that deeper relationship with Him. God's Word is clear about this fact. Luke 11: 9-10 (KJV) says, "And I say unto you, Ask, and it shall be given:

seek, and ye shall find; knock and it shall be opened unto you. For everyone that asketh; receiveth; and he that seeketh findeth; and to him that knocketh it shall be opened."

Three great examples of forgiveness in the Bible include Esau and Jacob (Gen.33:4), Joseph and his brothers (Gen. 50:19) and Jesus on the cross (Luke 23:34) Forgiveness unlocks anger, bitterness and resentment. Its sets us on a road to healing and ultimately draw us closer to God and glorifies Him. In all the Biblical examples of forgiveness, God's kingdom was advanced. People were set free and the miraculous occurred. The benefits of forgiving always outnumber the results of forgiveness. We forgive because we must; the alternative is bondage. We forgive because we love and obey Christ to bless and not curse others. We cannot truly forgive someone without the power of Jesus Christ. It starts with Him. Forgiveness is inevitable when you rely on and involve God in the process (Jayson).

This answer by Jesus makes it clear that forgiveness is not easy for us. It is not a one-time choice and then we automatically live in a state of forgiveness. It may require a lifetime of forgiving, but it is important to the Lord. We must continue forgiving until the matter is settled in our heart. It must be known there can be no end to our Christian duty to forgive. In fact, if we try to keep record of the times we have forgiven, we have not forgiven at all. When we continually keep a record of forgiving, we continually keep a record of the wrongs as well. This is contrary to the entire biblical concept of forgiveness which is to let go, and to leave it in God's hands (Richardson).

Chapter 7

The Power of Forgiving Others

Joyce Meyer suggests we need to forgive the way God tells us to. God says in His word that we need to pray for our enemies even if we do not really want them to be blessed. Often, after we have prayed for God to bless them, the first thing that God blesses them with is the revelation of what they have done. She said you cannot have the right relationship with Him if you do not admit what you have done and come to a place of truth in your life.

God desires truth in the inner being (Psalm 51). You must face the truth about where you are. God asks us to pray, not curse, but speak well of and not speak evil of that person. He said pray in obedience to God and decides to stop talking about them. Even if we still feel like we are angry, it does not necessarily mean that we have not forgiven them. Leave it at God's feet.

When we obey God, no matter how we feel, it breaks the enemy's power over us. When we take the step of obedience, God gives us power and a blessing for that act of obedience. When we do right, even if you feel all wrong about it that is when you are growing spiritually. It is time to overcome evil with good. "Do not be overcome by evil but overcome evil with good" (Romans 12:21 KJV).

Being forgiving to yourself and others can protect against stress and the toll it takes on mental health, according to a new study in the Journal of Health Psychology. Researchers looked at the effects of lifetime stress on a person's mental health, and how more forgiving people fared compared to people who were not so forgiving. Toussaint asked 148 young adults to fill out questionnaires that assessed their levels of lifetime stress, their tendency to forgive and their mental and physical health. Researchers also found that people with greater exposure to stress over their lifetime had worse mental and physical health. In people that were highly forgiving of both themselves and others, this characteristic alone virtually eliminated the connection between stress and mental illness. The sample of people in the study was small, and more research is needed to fully understand the benefit of being more forgiving. Toussaint says he believes "100 %" that forgiveness can be learned. Toussaint stated that many therapists are now working to cultivate forgiveness into their sessions.

According to an article in the January issue of Harvard Women's Health Watch, forgiving those who hurt you can improve your mental and physical wellbeing. This article lists five reasons to forgive and defines what forgiveness is and is not. It also provides an exercise to help you learn to forgive. It may come as a surprise that forgiving is a skill you can hone, and that granting forgiveness may do more for you than the person you forgive. Harvard Women's Watch discusses the following five positive health effects of forgiving that have been scientifically studied:

Reduced stress. Researchers found that mentally nursing a grudge puts your body through the same strains as a major stressful event: Muscles tense, blood pressure rises, and sweating increases.

Better heart health. One study found a link between forgiving someone for a betrayal and improvements in blood pressure and heart rate, and a decreased workload for the heart.

Stronger relationships. A 2004 study showed that women who could forgive their spouses and feel benevolent toward them resolved conflicts more effectively.

Reduced pain. A small study on people with chronic back pain found that those who practiced meditation focusing on converting anger to compassion felt less pain and anxiety than those who received regular care.

Greater happiness. When you forgive someone, you make yourself, rather than the person who hurt you, responsible for your happiness. One survey showed that people who talk about forgiveness during psychotherapy sessions experience greater improvements than those who do not.

Our forgiveness of each other has more to do with an attitude than a specific act. Jackson suggests some principles which highlight the sort of temperament that one must cultivate if he would be Christ-like (Luke 23:34).

The forgiving person does not attempt to take revenge upon those who have wronged him (Romans 12:17).

The forgiving person does not hate the offender; rather, despite the person's evil, he loves (agape) him still.

The forgiving person is kindly disposed and tenderhearted toward his adversary (Ephesians 4:32).

The forgiving person is approachable; he leaves the door for reconciliation wide open and longs for the welfare of the transgressor.

The forgiving person is not merely passive in waiting for the offender to repent; he actively seeks the repentance of the one who wronged him (Matthew 18:15-17).

Forgiveness must be done from the heart if we want God to pardon us (Matthew 18:35). There is a difference in lip or verbal forgiveness and heart forgiveness. Heart forgiveness must be given unconditionally and is Godward and vertical. With the help of God, the victim seeks to set aside bitterness, hatred, and revenge. Heart forgiveness restores the victim. It removes the evil thoughts that undermine communion and fellowship with God. Heart forgiveness is the required response to all offenses. It can be done alone before God in prayer, done continually, and done without verbal forgiveness. Lip or verbal forgiveness is conditional, is manward and horizontal. The victim responds to the repentance of the offender by telling him that he is forgiven. Verbal forgiveness restores the offender. It renews fellowship and makes full reconciliation possible. Verbal forgiveness is required only when the offender repents, and communicated to the offender, requires the repentance of the offender, so it is not always doable. It is required only once, and it means nothing without heart forgiveness. To be genuine, forgiveness must come from the heart. Certainly, when the offender repents, the Christian must verbally forgive him. But this means nothing unless the Christian has already forgiven from the heart and has determined that he will continue to forgive from the heart (Wright).

In the Bible, the heart is the essence of the personality. In the book *The Bible Doctrine of Man* C. Ryder Smith describes the heart as the seat of the intellect, of the will, and of feeling. Wright says modern thinking associated the heart with the emotions; this is different from the way the word heart is used in the Bible. In the Bible, the heart is not separated from the intellect. Rather, according to   Smith, "In the New Testament, it is the heart, not the head, that rules the body, and it is in the heart that Christ 'dwells.'"

C.S. Lewis said, "Real forgiveness means looking steadily at the sin, the sin that is left over without any excuse, after all allowances have been made, and seeing it in all its horror, dirt, meanness and malice, and nevertheless being wholly reconciled to the man who has done it" (*The Business of Heaven*, p. 62).

Forgiveness means releasing resentment. Resentment is an inevitable result of being damaged and wounded by another person's words or actions. Dan Hamilton wrote "suppressed resentment will never die; it will be held in reserve and nurtured like malignant toadstools in the cellar. Resentment suppressed will never lose its power; like a spark in a gasoline tank, a bit of momentary friction will set off a resonating explosion" (*Forgiveness*, p. 6).

Forgiveness means choosing to love. You choose to seek the best for the other person even when you feel hurt and angry. It is to deal with others as Christ has dealt with us. If you are a forgiven person, you can be a forgiving person. First Corinthians 13:4 reminds us that "love keeps no record of wrongs." The word "record" is an accountant's term. We put things down to remember them or to keep a tally on them. True forgiveness remembers to forget. Forgiveness means trusting God to work in you and in the other person. God deals in justice and in grace. He does that in us and in others. God chooses to work through forgiveness. Forgiveness means ceasing to feel resentment for wrongs and offenses done toward us. It includes pardon and the restoration of broken relationships. Forgiveness is the act of renouncing anger and ill feelings against others.

The greatest forgiveness of all is an act of God, by which He releases sinners from judgment and frees us from the divine penalty levied because of our sins. But forgiveness is also a human act toward one's fellow human beings. God's forgiveness, because of the death of Christ on our behalf, is to become an incentive for us to forgive others who offend us.

In Matthew chapter eighteen, Peter had learned from his traveling with Jesus the importance of forgiving. Peter had a question about the frequency of forgiveness. He said to Jesus, "How often shall my brother sin against me, and I forgive him?" Forgiveness is one of the highest of human virtues, because it reflects the character of God. God has freely forgiven us, and He expects the same from us toward others. Jesus taught that Christian compassion forgives repeatedly.

Jesus had taught us to always have a spirit of forgiveness. We should never be slow to forgive even the smallest infractions committed against us. Forgiveness should have no limits. Every one of us is indebted to God. He forgives when we repent but only if we practice forgiveness towards others. If we hold grudges and malice and bitter feelings toward other persons, we had better quickly take some steps toward making peace.

Forgiveness should make us generous towards those who wrong us. God has forgiven every one of us a great debt of sin, and therefore we should graciously forgive those who offend us. Ephesians 4:32 says we are to be kind and tender-hearted, forgiving one another even as God has forgiven us. It is this awareness of the tremendous cost of our forgiveness that keeps us from refusing to forgive those who mistreat us. Failure to forgive others will bring terrible consequences. We must consider what unforgiveness does to us. It can cause mental and physical problems including nervous breakdown, stress, elevated blood pressure, and ulcerated stomach. Forgiveness must be a constant attitude. Forgiveness is a blessing God bestows upon those who accept Christ.

The benefits of forgiving are recently being discovered by science and have long been taught by religious organizations. Scientifically validated benefits of forgiving include the reduction of chronic pain, cardiovascular problems, and violent behavior; increased hope; and decreased levels of depression and anxiety. People who do not forgive typically have higher heart rates and blood pressure along with other physical problems. The unforgiving responses of blame, anger, and hostility have been linked with poor health, particularly coronary disease and even premature death. Most people who have forgiven others will testify of the joy experienced as the emotional burden they had been carrying was released (Rowden, Davis).

When we forgive others, there is a freedom where we are no longer shackled by our own anger. It moves us from our selfish illusions to a beautiful reality. It is hard work. But letting go of the fantasies that we can change the past, that we can change others, or even that we are the ones who can change ourselves opens room for God to help us ward off the resentment we feel. Each time we forgive, it paves the way for the next time we need to forgive. Practicing the courage and patience and letting the Lord into the process of forgiveness becomes like exercising a muscle. It grows stronger and stronger. Together with Him we can come to a point where forgiveness is intuitive, a blessed way to live (Blair).

When we forgive others, we must remember that every person's sense of worth is important. Realize that by forgiving them you aid in their personal experiences of forgiveness. Develop empathy and emotional understanding for the situation of your offender. Seek with all your heart and mind for anger to be lifted. This may often include prayer, meditation, or some other activity to rid you from anger's poison.

Remember that forgiving rarely entails memory loss but freedom from preoccupation with the offense. Do not let your thoughts, emotions, and reactions be consumed by the offense (Rowden).

Forgiveness researchers suggest that family members from all families must humbly seek and grant forgiveness so that their relationships can survive. Forgiving one another from the heart helps restore the peace and contentment that can be a part of every family. But forgiveness is a gift you give yourself. By forgiving another, regardless of the actions of others, you do yourself a great service. You let go of bitterness, contempt, vindictiveness, and desires for revenge that sap you of mental and emotional energy you could use in other areas of your life. It is important to let these things go because if you do not, the other person, even if you never see them again, continues to hold power over your emotions and your thoughts and you (Davis).

Patience is important during the process of forgiveness. The promise is that forgiveness is possible. Even when the hurt seems too great to repair, God tells us, "I will remove from them their heart of stone and give them a heart of flesh" (Ezekiel 11:19). We experience a heart of stone when we are too angry, too selfish, or too frozen by the pain others have caused us. A heart of flesh, while it may be vulnerable, is compassionate. A heart of flesh sees that while we are feeling pain, the other person may also be hurting for that pain they caused us. We can get so caught up in ourselves that we do not even notice another is struggling from the offense. It is true that people need to be held accountable for their actions, but these people also need patience from us. As it was said, "Be patient with me" (Matthew 18:26). Practicing patience with another, holding onto the hope and vision for our relationship with them, is a true act of compassion. We need to invite the Lord into the journey and ask for the courage it takes for us to be patient with another and the understanding needed to see that they, too, are working through the pain that needs forgiveness.

Forgiveness does not demand you forget the experience. It does not mean you are condoning what happened or minimizing the offense. It will not make you look weak or vulnerable. In fact, if possible and appropriate, you can clearly express the impact the harmful actions had on you. Your forgiveness does not depend on the offender deserving it, asking for it, or expressing remorse. It does not mean reconciling or trusting if there is no sign of change or sincere regret (Davis).

If you think of forgiveness as a benevolent emotion, you might never be able to feel it for an offender. But there is another form of forgiveness where the negative emotional charge is replaced with matter-of-fact acceptance and indifference. It is based on a rational and realistic assessment of the painful incident, how it came about, and each person's role in it. This is often enough to release the negative bondage to the perpetrator/offender, so they no longer play a role in your present and future life.

Chapter 8

The Steps of Forgiveness

1. Tell your story. Describe what happened. Acknowledge that an offense has taken place and assign responsibility appropriately. Clearly identify the person(s) who caused you harm.

2. Acknowledge the pain you are feeling. It may fluctuate, rise in intensity or recede into the background. Do not try to suppress your emotions. But also, do not disappear into them. Witness your feelings and hang in there until they subside. Watch and challenge your thoughts connected with the feelings. Are they rational or dramatizing the situation? Are they true and realistic or merely loud and insistent? Are they making you feel worse or helping your emotional release?

3. Understand what happened. Why might the other person have behaved the way they did? What is their story? Was the offense intentionally directed at you or was it a result of their own failure? Did they set out to hurt you or were you in the wrong place at the wrong time with the wrong people?

4. Tell the story differently. Without condoning the offense, use your new perspective to reframe the experience with greater understanding and detachment.

5. Create closure. Use whatever gives you a sense of completion. Write a letter, create a ritual that symbolizes your shift, and celebrate your new perspective by doing something special you enjoy.

Acknowledge that you had the strength and courage to extend forgiveness to someone who may or may not deserve it, and that it no longer matters. Forgiveness is about you, not them. The most important part is achieving your own inner freedom, whether it is based on compassion or neutral acceptance (Burscheid).

Sometimes it is easier to forgive the actions of another person than your own transgression or mistake. But there is no benefit to self-condemnation. It does not change anything. Only choosing different behaviors or making amends for your actions will make a difference for the future. For self-forgiveness you need to extend compassion, understanding and patience to oneself to grow into a better person. You must realize that it's up

to you whether you accept stagnation or move forward
in life.

Chapter 9

How Forgiveness Can Change Your Life

Forgiveness aids psychological healing through positive changes, and in effect, improves physical and mental health. It restores a victim's sense of personal power and helps bring about reconciliation between the offended and offender. Additionally, it promotes hope for the resolution of real intergroup conflicts (Fincham).

In our personal lives, our attitudes are much more guaranteed to have an impact than in the more distant chaos of the political world. Forgiveness concerning those around us is guaranteed to improve how we feel about ourselves, and it may have a good impact on others as well.

Forgiving ourselves allows us to recognize our own faults and then to correct them as much as we can without languishing in unforgiving guilt and shame. Guilt and shame make us less able to examine ourselves. We try to relieve these self-punishing attitudes by denying responsibility for any wrong actions. In a state of denial that protects us from guilt and shame, we cannot identity what we need change about ourselves.

Further, regarding ourselves, forgiving others is to make peace within ourselves. We give up anger and resentment and thereby become freer of spiritually corrupting malice. We no longer give those who have hurt us the power to continue to do so by preoccupying us with their deeds (Breggin).

Forgiveness can relieve us of the motivation to gratuitously harm others. We may still feel the necessity of taking self-protective actions that end up harming others, for example, by excluding them from our lives, but we have not done so out of malice. We have acted to protect ourselves or our families and not for inflicting harm (Breggin).

Researchers and scientists have discovered the health benefits of attaining forgiveness. Their studies have shown that serious mental, emotional and physical consequences can result from holding on to grudges and bitterness. Consequences such as depression, anxiety and the feeling that your life lacks meaning and purpose, as well as the loss of valuable connectedness with family and friends become high prices to pay for holding on to the hurt. Forgiveness can help rebuild your life, restore trust, empower a positive attitude toward others and reconcile with the Lord.

Forgiveness is incredibly powerful. If it could be bottled, a daily dose would probably save many marriages. Researchers found that the health benefits of forgiveness seem to come largely from the ability to reduce negative effects (feelings of tension, anger, depression and fatigue). With forgiveness, the victim relinquishes ideas of revenge, and feels less hostile, angry, or upset about the experiences, the University of Tennessee researchers found. The study suggests that this pathway most fully mediates the forgiveness-health relationship. Thus, the health consequences of lack of forgiveness may be carried by increased levels of negative emotion.

One researcher at Baylor University stated that one barrier people face in forgiving themselves is that they feel they deserve to feel bad. The study found that making amends gives us permission to let go, and live and forgive oneself. Another study has shown that forgiveness lowered the blood pressure. A 2011 study of married couples in the journal Personal Relationship, for instance, showed that when the victim in the situation forgave the other person, both experienced a decrease in blood pressure. "This study provides the first evidence we are aware of suggesting that receiving forgiveness also predicts positive physiological functioning: Perpetrators who received more conciliatory behavior (as reported by victims) had lower blood pressure than did perpetrators who received less," researchers wrote in the study.

Research presented at a 2011 meeting of the Society of Behavioral Medicine showed that people with HIV who practiced genuine forgiveness toward someone who had hurt them had higher CD4 cell percentages (considered positive for their immune status), Medscape reported.

True Christian ministry must involve forgiveness, and those who embrace true forgiveness experience lower levels of stress, anxiety, and depression. They will have a greater likelihood of experiencing significant posttraumatic growth. Even in situations where the possibility of forgiveness may seem remote, research indicates there is hope.

Researchers have found that female victims of spousal emotional abuse have considerable improvements in depression, anxiety, self-esteem, and posttraumatic stress after forgiving the abuser. The study shows that the benefits of forgiveness in general were significant; it was the specific sense of feeling forgiven by God that produced the greatest health-related improvement. Three related dimensions of forgiveness were examined, finding that feeling forgiven by God had the strongest forgiveness-related health mediating effect, while self-forgiveness and forgiveness of others also contributed to the positive physical health effects of religiosity (Aponte).

Chapter 10

Helping Others to Forgive

The first step in helping another person to forgive is admitting fault. If the person has already told you that he or she is self-condemning, a large part of the battle is won. Those so called "self-conscious emotions" are already out in the open. Confession to God is essential, and it can encourage the person. The person already knows in his or her head (and perhaps heart) that confessing promotes healing. Often, the problem is that the person has confessed repeatedly and still does not feel that God has, or will, or is able to forgive them. You cannot force the person to feel less guilt and shame by anything you say, so the experience of God's forgiveness and the release it creates must often be lived into. Do not fight a battle you cannot win trying to make a person "feel forgiven."

When helping others to commit to virtuous living, battling self-condemnation can take a real toll on body and mind. Trying to control moods or negative thoughts literally uses up the glucose in the brain. There is a physical basis for lowered self-control after one has exerted a lot of willpower. People should not go from battling self–condemnation directly to striving with all their might to be ultra-virtuous. People need recovery and a period of healing. People must accept that we are all flawed and need help finding our way sometimes. Christians usually know the Christian doctrine that God forgives them because Jesus died for them and that Jesus would have died for them if they had been the only person in the world. Yet, knowing this as doctrine and believing it with heartfelt attachment and then, even more, believing it could apply to them are not the same sometimes. It helps to encourage people to seek whether they can see any benefit in what they did. Without trying to justify what they did, they can often see the hand of God working in the event to bring about some good.

Forgiving others is sometimes very hard, but it is essential if you want to break out of the bondage that it has brought you under. Forgiving others opens you up for the Lord to begin healing your soul (inner healing). Since forgiveness blocks us from receiving God's forgiveness of our sins (Matthew 6:15), it puts up a wall between us and the source of our healing.

If you have a hard time forgiving others, it is because the love of Christ is not flowing through you.

You can solve this problem by working on your relationship with your heavenly Father, so you can come to know of His great love for you, and then your spirit will respond, and His love will begin to flow through you naturally. When that begins to happen, forgiving those who have wronged you will become much easier.

Forgiving others may seem to be a choice, and in one sense, it is a choice, but God has been very clear about forgiveness. He has given us specific direction in numerous Scriptures, all of which can be summed up in just one word: Forgive. He is not talking about what is in the best interest of the person who needs to be forgiven. We are the ones who God is trying to protect. We are the ones who receive the most benefit from forgiveness, not the other person. A spirit of unforgiveness complicates and compromises our daily walk with God. Forgiving others releases us from anger and allows us to receive the healing we need. The whole reason God has given us specific direction is that He does not want anything to stand between Him and us. God's love for us is beyond our comprehension. Forgiving others spares us from the consequences of living with an unforgiving heart (Worthington).

Without forgiveness, we remain tethered to the person who harmed us. We are bound with chains of bitterness, tied together, trapped. Until we can forgive the person who harmed us, that person will hold the key to our happiness; that person will be our jailor. When we forgive, we take back control of our own fate and our feelings. We become our own liberators. We do not forgive to help the other person. We forgive for ourselves. We must help others to forgive, by being caring, compassionate, and having a forgiving spirit toward them. It is important for us to embrace what Jesus has done for us and extend that in thoughts, words, and deeds toward others with the essence of forgiveness. In forgiving one another, we draw on the forgiveness that Jesus has given us by deciding to release another from the penalty of sin. He puts it as simply as possible, forgiveness is releasing the other from the penalty of sin, so the relationship can be restored (Smith).

Understanding forgiveness as a decision to let go is important because we often confuse forgiveness with our emotions. When this happens, forgiveness ebbs and flows as our emotions fluctuate. When we do not feel angry, we think we have forgiven, but when anger resurfaces, it seems we are back at square one. Just when we think an issue has been laid to rest for good, it can pop up again. While forgiveness effects and can bring relief to our emotions, it is much more than an emotion. It is a decision we make based on our worship of God to forgive as He forgives. God's forgiveness is not a declaration of emotion but a declaration that His people are forgiven and pardoned from their sins just as a judge would dismiss a case from a courthouse. In that sense, forgiveness is a decision we must make to move forward in life.

Joyce Meyer says we can help ourselves and others by releasing them so God can do what only He can do. If we are in the way, trying to get revenge or take care of the situation ourselves instead trusting and obeying God, He has no obligation to deal with that person. However, God will deal with those who hurt us if we will put them in His hands through forgiveness. The act of forgiving is our seed of obedience to His word. Once we have sown our seed, He is faithful to bring a harvest of blessing to us one way or another.

Another way that forgiveness can help us is that we release God to do His work in us. We will be happier and feel better physically when we are not filled with the poison of unforgiveness. Serious diseases can develop because of the stress and pressure that bitterness, resentment and unforgiveness put on a person. Mark 11:22-26 clearly teaches us that unforgiveness hinders our faith from working. The Father cannot forgive our sins if we do not forgive other people. We reap what we sow. Sow mercy, and you will reap mercy; sow judgement, and reap judgement. So, do yourself a favor, and forgive.

There are still more benefits of forgiveness. Your fellowship with God flows freely when you are willing to forgive, but it gets blocked by unforgiveness. Forgiveness also keeps Satan from getting an advantage over you (2 Corinthians 2:10-11).

Ephesians 4:26-27 tells us not to let the sun go down on our anger or give the devil any such foothold or opportunity. Meyer said remember the devil must have a foothold before he can get a stronghold. Do not help Satan torture you. Be quick to forgive.

Chapter 11

Various Descriptions of Forgiveness

Decisional forgiveness is largely external; it is a change in the way you behave toward someone who has wronged you, even though you may still feel negatively toward the person. True forgiveness, on the other hand, is an internal change in the way you feel toward this person with resentment giving way to positive emotions like empathy, sympathy, compassion, and even love. This is the real kind of forgiveness; the other one is the much more common play-acting variety (Canup).

Unconditional forgiveness is a different model of forgiveness than a gift with strings attached. This is forgiveness as a grace, a gift, freely given. In this model, forgiveness frees the person who inflicted the harm from the weight of the victim's whim, what the victim may demand to grant forgiveness, and the victim's threat of vengeance. However, it also frees the one who forgives. The one who offers forgiveness as a grace is immediately untethered from the yoke that bound him or her to the person who caused the harm. When you forgive, you are free to move on in life, to grow, and to no longer be a victim. When you forgive, your future is unshackled from your past (Tutu).

Forgiveness of Love is a Christian perspective on forgiveness derived from the New Testament. It emphasizes the moral necessity of responding to the wrongdoing by accepting it, turning the other cheek, and embracing the offender in an act of love or compassion. One recent interpretation combines forgiveness as love with a conception of forgiveness as absolution, an overall process of reconciliation between wrongdoer and victim (Biggar).

Forgiveness as a virtue is another type of forgiveness found within the western monotheistic and philosophical traditions. Forgiveness has often been regarded as a "high" and difficult virtue and the opposite, unwillingness to forgive, as a vice. Yet this poses an immediate problem of interpretation, namely, whether forgiveness is a "high" virtue in the sense that while it is morally laudable it is beyond duty. Since supererogatory actions are permissible, not obligatory, it follows that a failure, at least in circumstances where forgiving would be supererogatory, would not, contrary to the ancient view, be a vice. In such view forgiveness is a virtue, or it is at least closely aligned with one or more of the traditional virtues such as magnanimity or sympathy. In ancient Greek thought, the views of Plato and Aristotle, the relationship between anger and living virtuously are noteworthy as is the Christian traditions' understanding of forgiveness as love or compassion.

People who practice conditional forgiveness, in other words, people who can only forgive if others say sorry first or promise not to do the transgression again, may be more likely to die earlier compared with people who are less likely to practice conditional forgiveness, according to a 2011 study in the *Journal of Behavioral Medicine*.

Dr. Monica A. Franks (2011) made the distinction between different paths to forgiveness because each situation varies and does not have the same opportunities in every situation. Therefore, we may have to pursue different means to achieve forgiveness. True forgiveness comes when a person can pursue true remorse on their part as a transgressor. This is often the easiest path to forgiveness because the other person admits faults, takes responsibility for their actions, and asks for forgiveness. In this situation, we may need to determine the sincerity of their apology, but otherwise we are able to allow ourselves to focus on resolving the emotions.

When this type of situation does occur, we are to feel our emotions and arrive at an understanding, such as recognizing that the other person did not hurt us intentionally or that they are truly trying to make amends and changing the behavior that caused the problem. Even if the person is remorseful, we cannot just move to forgiveness without a release of our emotions. We need to feel the anger and the sadness. This will help us to process the hurt and release the emotions and more quickly reach a resolution.

Acceptance forgiveness is another type of path in forgiveness. In the situations where the transgressor does not feel remorse it is even more difficult to achieve forgiveness. How do you pardon an offense when the person does not show remorse and is not trying to remedy the situation? This could be a situation where the person may lack awareness that they hurt you, or a person may have hurt you due to some personal limitations such as mental illness or ignorance. Many times, the transgressor does not ever recognize their mistakes. In this case, we need to deal with forgiveness without an apology or change in behavior. The reason it is called "acceptance forgiveness" is because we need to be able to let go of the resentment even if we cannot pardon the offense. We still need to release the anger, pain, and sadness. However, we may need to do this through indirect means such as writing about our feelings or talking to a trusted friend.

Resolution means coming to an acceptance that although you have been wronged, you can move on in your life and not dwell on what was done to you. Usually, by the time you have released your emotions, you are ready to do this. Therefore, the key is to fully experience and release the emotions.

Why Forgiveness Is Important

Principled Forgiveness is one of the most difficult. It is called for when we are faced with transgressions which are deliberate and are meant to hurt us, or sometimes people hurt us repeatedly or even derive pleasure from hurting us. In these situations, it requires the path of principled forgiveness which means we need to find a higher level of understanding to forgive. It is called "principled" based upon Kohlberg's theory of moral reasoning in which we decide upon our moral actions not because we will have punished or rewarded and not because of the impact upon the people, but because we believe in a higher ethical standard of how to behave.

When Jesus was dying on the cross he said, "Father, forgive them, for they know not what they do." I think he exhibited principled forgiveness in this respect. However, Jesus also asked, "Why have you forsaken me?" This demonstrates the grief process in which he released his emotions. The emotion of despair is combined anger and sadness. Too often, people want to emulate Jesus in his ability to forgive without realizing that he engaged in the full grief process of releasing his emotions as well. They try to forgive without the release of emotions which only keeps them stuck in the process.

Direct forgiveness, in contrast, should be more frequently used by couples who are dating because direct forgiveness is marked by discussion of transgression and its potential meaning to the relationship (Waldron &Kelley, 2005). Kelley (1998) suggested transgressions may be particularly meaningful in the context of dating because transgressions can often signal the need for reevaluation of the relationship. Dating partners may have more room for relational de-escalation than friends following transgressions and may need to explicitly discuss transgressions to best approximate the appropriate level of commitment to the relationship (Foley & Fraser, 1998). Frank discussion about transgressions, moreover, may be necessary for the long-term stability of relationships with unresolved conflict and serial arguing (K.L. Johnson & Roloff, 2000).

Chapter 12

Impact of Forgiveness

Forgiveness, however, can be a problem for many people simply because they are not clear about what forgiveness really is. All too often forgiveness gets confused with reconciliation, a larger process of which forgiveness is but one part. John 1: 9 says, "If we confess our sins, he is faithful and just to forgive us our sins, and to cleanse us from all unrighteousness."

To receive forgiveness, we must first recognize that we have sinned, confess our sins, and then believe upon Jesus for the forgiveness of our sins and that therefore He died on the cross. He did this so that we might be forgiven (Matthew 26-28). Without the blood which Jesus shed on the cross, there is no forgiveness for our sins (Hebrews 9:22).

We forgive because Christ forgave us. (Col. 3:13, Ephes. 4:32) Jesus commands us to forgive. He confirms this in the daily prayer when "He taught us to pray, and forgive us our debts, as we forgive our debtors" (Matt. 6:9-13). We must go in prayer, confess ours sins, and ask for His forgiveness. Jesus also said, "For if you forgive men their trespasses, your Father will also forgive you" (Matt. 6:15). So we must forgive so God will forgive us when we sin. We forgive so we do not give the devil any power (2 Cor. 10-11). Jesus talked about the need for Christians to forgive others and how God hates the wicked sin of unforgiveness (Matthew 18:21-35). 1 John 3:15 says, "Whoever hates his brother is a murderer." Hatred is unforgiveness. Unforgiveness sin is bondage (NIV).

We forgive so we do not get entangled by the bondage. (Gal. 5: 1) We forgive because it is the right thing to do. Life without forgiveness and forgiving is unbearable. We forgive because it helps bring healing and restoration to us. We cannot do this unless we forgive as we have been forgiven. We (Christians) are told to be merciful and above all, to love. "Therefore, as the elect of God, holy and beloved, put on tender mercies, kindness, humility, meekness and longsuffering; (Col 3:12) bearing with one another, and forgiving one another. If anyone has a complaint against another forgive as Christ forgave you, so you must do." But above all things put on love, which is the bond of peace. (Col 3:14) We are then free to "let the peace of God rule in your hearts, to which also you were called in one body, thankful." (Col. 3:15).

God hates sin; He cannot stand to look at its ugliness. Therefore, unconfessed sin in our lives comes between us and damages our relationship with the Lord. Not only does unforgiveness come between us and God, it also breaks our relationships with others. Because God hate sins, the price for forgiveness is high.

Scripture gives the following requirements for forgiveness: *Sacrifice.* Hebrews 9:22 says that "without the shedding of blood, there is no forgiveness." *Forgiveness of others.* 1 Corinthians 13:5 says that "real love keeps no record of wrongs." Proverbs 17:9 tells us that a real friend will forgive. God has also made forgiving others a requirement for receiving His forgiveness. "Be kind to one another, forgiving each other, just as in Christ, God forgave you." (Ephesians 4:32). *Confession of your sins.* We must admit our sins to God if our relationship with Him is to be restored completely. Looking back at the real need for forgiveness, we see that unconfessed sin can separate us in our relationship with God. Confession is the way to restore that relationship with the Lord, remembering that it is for our own benefit that we confess to return to the Lord because He is faithful even when we are not (2 Timothy 2:13). "If we confess our sins, He is faithful and just to forgive our sins and purify us from all unrighteousness." *Repentance.* We must decide to change, to turn from our sins. "Therefore, this is what the Lord says, 'if you repent, I will restore you that you may serve me'" (Jeremiah 15: 19). Is kind to one another, tenderhearted, forgiving one another, as God in Christ forgave you? When believers forgive others in a biblical manner, they demonstrate their love for the Lord by being obedient to His Word (1 John 5:3). When believers forgive, their love for the Lord is evidenced and their love for others is demonstrated in their life (1 John 4:20-21). Believers who obey God's Word by forgiving others also have the potential for a vibrant and productive prayer life. Believers display the difference Jesus has made in their lives when they forgive biblically.

Forgiveness allows you to live in an intimate, long-term relationship with another sinner. Forgiveness is the only way to negotiate through the weakness and failure that will daily mark your relationships. It is the only way to deal with hurt and disappointment. Forgiveness is the only way to have hope and confidence restored. It is the only way to protect your love and reinforce the unity that you have built. Forgiveness is the only way not to be kidnapped by the past. It is the only way to give your relationships the blessing of fresh starts and new beginnings.

Chapter 13

God and Forgiveness

Daniel 9:9 says, "To the Lord our God belong mercy and forgiveness, for we have rebelled against Him." Our awesome Father in Heaven was the creator of forgiveness, and so it belongs to Him and He lavishes us with it abundantly every day. God knew from the beginning of time all the sins that would take place. He carried the burden of love that only the Father could carry.

God forgives freely anyone who comes to Him; you must know how to receive forgiveness. Forgiveness does not just come from God but also from His flock. Luke 17:3-4 says, "So watch yourselves" If your brother sins, rebuke him, and if he repents, forgive him, and if he sins against you seven times in the day, and turns to you seven times, saying, 'I repent,' you must forgive him." This is not always easy. If repentance is genuine, it must always be forgiven, even if it is the same sin repeatedly. Human nature wants to push us in a direction of giving up on someone who is in perpetual sin because we tend to stop believing in someone who is constantly engaged in sin, but the Bible is clear on this issue. God never gives up on His children who come in His name to ask for forgiveness, which is why we cannot give up either (Hill).

For true forgiveness to take place, one must completely remove pride. A proud heart will never truly forgive. Matthew 6:14 says, "For if you forgive others their trespasses, your heavenly Father will also forgive you, but if you do not forgive others their trespasses, neither will your Father forgive your trespasses." This really does sum up a prideful heart. You absolutely cannot expect to be forgiven if you are too proud to forgive someone else. Pride has no place in a Christian's heart.

Forgiving brings us closer to God. We should be in communion with God to be able to forgive someone. When we step out past our pain to do so, we are reminded of exactly what God did for us when He sent His son to die for our sins. Forgiveness takes humility, and it is in a humble state of mind that we remember just how we were and are in God's forgiveness. As a result, we draw closer to Him and become more thankful for what He has done for us.

Why Forgiveness Is Important

In addition, when we are holding a grudge against someone, that person and whatever pain was inflicted on us consume a large amount of our thoughts and feeling, thereby leaving less room in our brain for God and His Word. Not to mention when we fill our head and heart with hatred and anger, it is kind of hard to fellowship with a loving, peaceful God because they do not go hand in hand. That is why Jesus told us to forgive others before we pray because He knows that if we do not, our heart really will not be in the right place to fellowship with Him! (Marrazzo)

Forgiving allows us to experience God's strength in our lives. In all honesty, forgiveness is hard. Forgiving someone who has done something extremely hurtful to us or someone we love does not come naturally, and it is in no way easy. Honestly, we cannot do it on our own. We must rely on God's strength to do it. Anytime we allow God's strength to work in our lives, wonderful things happen. When the power that raised Christ from the dead is working in you, there is no limit to how God can use you and bless you. "The Spirit of God, who raised Jesus from the dead, lives in you. Just as God raised Christ Jesus from the dead, he will give life to your mortal bodies by this same Spirit living within you" (Romans 8:11).

God's forgiveness brings happiness. When we know God's forgiveness, we are blessed (happy). "Blessed (happy) is he whose transgressions are forgiven, whose sins are covered. Blessed (happy) is the man whose sin the Lord does not count against him and in whose spirit is no deceit." (Psalm 32:1-2)(KJV).

God chooses not to hold our sins against us. Jesus covered our sins; God chooses to put them out of His mind. "I, even I am he who blots out your transgressions, for my own sake, and remembers your sins no more." (Isaiah 43:2) God removes our sins from us. "It is possible for the Lord to look at us without seeing our sins because when he forgave us, he removed our sins as far as the east to the west" (Psalm 103:12).

We can forgive ourselves. When we are forgiven, we can forgive ourselves and go on with our lives. "Brothers, I do not consider myself yet to have hold of it. But one thing I do: forgetting what is behind and straining toward what is ahead, I press on toward the goal to win the prize for which God has called me heavenward in Christ Jesus" (Philippians 3:13-14). (Christian Answers.Net)

God calls us to forgive. It is His will for us to obey His call. It is something extremely special which we are given, and something precious we are to replicate to others. It is not easy. It requires the practice of maturity, the patience to allow the process to unfold, and the tact to endure it. Forgiveness is also a mandate from the Lord. We can take great comfort in knowing that He is working while we are waiting, and even suffering. We can best practice forgiveness by realizing how much we have been forgiven. We can then be imitators of that forgiveness when others willfully or unknowingly cause us setback or harm. The magnitude of forgiveness from our Lord for what we have done can never measure up to anything others could do to us. When we put forgiveness into practice, we will be free from the bondage of bitterness and pain that imprisons us, disconnecting us from life and its wonders, which God has provided for us.

Chapter 14

Self-forgiveness

Once we use self-forgiveness, our inner door to love opens. It is quite magical. We are now able to feel the universal love and well-being that has been waiting beyond the door that we had kept closed within ourselves for so long. In truth, we have always had access to this healing love, but holding ourselves hostage by self-judgment kept us from feeling it. It is quite a delicious relief to feel the warmth washing in as we open to our own compassion and self-forgiveness. Self-forgiveness can open doors to all forms of abundance and well-being. It all comes through the same doorway. This includes not only a love for us, but loving connections and appreciation from other people, fulfilling experiences, avenues of expression for your unique gifts, money, etc. (Sherwood).

Self-forgiveness completely changes your energy field. As you begin practicing it, you align yourself with a higher, more loving source of energy. Then, by the Law of Attraction, as you are more loving toward yourself, you draw in circumstances and people who are also more loving toward you. The outer reflects the inner.

Self-forgiveness completely changes your "outer" reality. Whatever is in our internal reality gets projected into our "outer" life. Whenever you have a conflict with someone, that conflict is only with yourself. The other person is playing the role of a voice in your head. Self-love and self-forgiveness does not just happen once and then we are healed finally and permanently. We must choose it again and again in our lives as new layers of our being become unveiled for our healing. We must keep doing our part. Each time we choose love, we open our inner door to our Creator and feel alignment with the vast, unlimited energy field of light, love, compassion, forgiveness, healing and wellbeing that is always here and available to us (Tift).

It is important to learn how to forgive yourself. First work on the obvious areas in your life, experiences that you have had in your past which bring up feelings of shame or guilt. As you work on those, you will become aware of other, more subtle ways that you withhold love from yourself, judge yourself, and keep yourself separate from God. We must be aware of things we tell ourselves about self. Our work is to bring awareness, love and self-forgiveness to these places inside ourselves (Tift).

Accepting and talking about feelings of remorse, regret, guilt and shame due to violating our own values is important. We must know our values and when there has been a breach to one of them. When people complain and object to our behavior, it does not translate into the fact that we did something wrong. Wrong action is determined by our values and not by the disapproval of others. However, we can use the disapproval of others to check out whether we acted in opposition to one of our values (Tift).

Moving out of a fixation on self-incrimination is an important process to enlarge our vision of how we came to make the choice we did.

Restitution and/or making amends. Is there some compensation to be offered to the injured party in the way of service, money or the replacement of damaged property? Someone making amends can be helpful in support of forgiving ourselves. An amend is an apology (expression of regret) accompanied by a commitment to refrain from the adverse behavior. An amend is not offered if it would create greater harm to either the injured party or the person making the amends.

Accept that being fully alive means making mistakes. This calls for a level of humility, allowing us

to be more accepting of our limits and letting go of
perfectionistic aspirations.

Acknowledge that forgiveness is the restoration
of our essential goodness and therefore it is our
fundamental responsibility. We become willing to let
go of the expectation that others are responsible to
forgive us, or that our self-forgiveness is dependent
upon being forgiven by another (Worthington).

Worthington says forgiving yourself and
breaking free from your past is never easy, but can be
achieved through these steps:

Receive Forgiveness from the Universe. Take
a step back and look at the big picture, not just those
guilt-inspiring moments of your life. Remind yourself
that everyone makes mistakes, and that you, too,
deserve to be forgiven. If you have a spiritual practice,
revisiting your teaching and growing your connection
with your beliefs can also help you let go.

**Repent and Repair Relationships That Were
Damaged.** For example, if you continue to feel guilt
over causing a traffic accident, pay it forward by
advocating for better safety precautions.

Reduce Rumination. Giving past failures less
time and attention is one way to help move forward.
Examine the expectations and standards you hold for

yourself. If you would forgive a friend for something, why hold a higher bar to clear for yourself?

Act Out a Ritual of Self-Forgiveness. Recall the hurt this situation has caused. Then actually give yourself the empathy you would give someone else, along with an altruistic gift of self-forgiveness. It may help to go through a ritual of forgiveness.

Embrace Self-Acceptance. Even after you have forgiven yourself, you may have a hard time coming to terms with your past mistakes. Accept what you cannot change. Remind yourself that actions do not define who you are.

Resolve to Live with More Care. We all make mistakes. By vowing not to repeat them, you will have an easier time making amends with what's been done while being hopeful about what's to come.

Ask for help. It can be very important to turn to a friend, mentor, counselor or member of the clergy whom we trust for guidance toward authentic self-forgiveness. It is vital that the helper not attempt to minimize what we did to have us feeling more cheerful. Nor should the helper be prone to shaming us. Helpers need to offer the kind of support that leads us to hold a larger understanding of what we did while assisting us in interrupting any perfectionism (Dunion).

Dunion says being unskilled at self-forgiveness can leave us dependent upon others for our self-worth, being risk-adverse, haunted by guilt and shame, trapped in self-loathing and hoping that making mistakes will be minimized. Ultimately, becoming more effective at self-forgiveness is simply a way to remain responsible for our self-worth. It is also a large welcome to our humanity as we release perfectionistic ambitions and attend to the task of inner reconciliation.

Making peace with ourselves is not a self-absorbed activity. We typically live with more courage when we hold the faith that we will devotionally move toward self-forgiveness. A risk that might have unfavorable consequences is no longer paralyzing, as we can anticipate moving toward self-forgiveness. It is a freedom that can yield more depth and meaning in our relationships. When we are not defending a self-concept pummeled by guilt and self-incrimination, we become more generous with offering compassion to others. Forgiveness possesses a heart-opening quality that tempers resentment and vindictiveness, allowing us to be more receptive to seeking reconciliation with others. As we strive less for perfection, we discover a growing acceptance for the limits and shortcomings of others. There is an abiding honoring of the human condition reflected by our own lives and the lives of others (Dunion).

Self-forgiveness is more important than interpersonal forgiveness (Mills, 1995). Transgressors may be able to achieve self-forgiveness independently of its counterpart (Holmgren, 1998). Moreover, the process of self-forgiveness may be dispositional or one of many responses to transgressions that are (1) interpersonal (i.e. harm against others), (2) intrapersonal (i.e. offense against the self), and/or (3) spiritual (i.e. harm against higher power), which adds additional chameleon-like qualities to the construct (cf. Enright, 1996, Hall &Fincham, 2005; Hughes, 1994; McConnell & Dixon, in press).

Therefore, experiencing self-forgiveness does not represent just a mere facet of interpersonal forgiveness because it may take many unique forms depending on transgressors' personal characteristic, their transgression target(s), their core beliefs about self-forgiveness, and relationship determinants. For example, self-forgiveness in relation to self-inflicted transgressions may indeed be wholly intrapersonal at times (Hughes, 1994), but transgressors also may need unconditional positive regard from another to experience personal senses of forgiveness (Bauer et al., 1992; Bowman, 2005). Further, empathic feelings towards another, perceived forgiveness, and conciliatory behavior are not likely to play significant roles in forgiveness of self under wholly intrapersonal circumstances. As self-forgiveness continues to become an important topic in the research literature, we begin to understand more fully its multifaceted nature.

Interpersonal Forgiveness: Several definitions of forgiveness have been forwarded over the years, making it difficult to find a consensus definition amongst scholars (Enright & Fitzgibbons, 2000). The goal is to briefly identify some common themes in recent social scientific forgiveness scholarship.

Forgiveness is most often conceptualized and examined from victims' perspectives, rather than transgressors' (Thompson et al., 2005). Forgiveness, moreover, is often said to be a constructive relational process involving the release of negative effects attributed to transgressors' hurtful actions (Younger et al., 2004). A motivation-based view of forgiveness characterizes it as the lessened motivation to seek revenge and avoidance from a transgressor along with an increased motivation to seek relational repair (McCullough et al., 1988). Recent studies suggest forgiveness is motivated by factors such as relational commitment, love, empathy, fear of losing one's partner, and emotional involvement (Kelly, 1988; Younger et al., 2004).

The extant literature on forgiveness focuses largely on why individuals forgive and the subsequent effects of forgiveness on individuals and relational well-being. The literature, in contrast, offers limited insight into how individuals forgive (Waldron & Kelly, 2005). In reviewing past forgiveness research, Waldron and Kelly concluded, "These studies have in common an emphasis on the individuals' feelings and cognitions associated with forgiveness, rather than communication behaviors used to provoke, express, or manage them" (P.274).

Kelley (1998) suggested that to more fully understand the forgiveness process, researchers must focus on the dynamics of communicating forgiveness in daily interactions. Kelley's analysis of forgiveness narratives remains one of the only studies to date examining communication aspects of forgiveness. Kelley's work indicates individuals forgive in three ways. The first form is direct forgiveness in which forgivers clearly and plainly tell offenders they are forgiven (i.e. "I forgive you"), often in the context of discussion about the transgression. Kelley stated, "Direct strategies included discussing the nature of the issue and the forgiver telling the offender that he or she understands" (p.263).

The second form is indirect forgiveness, whereby individuals do not explicitly tell others they are forgiven; rather, forgiveness is "just understood" (Kelley, 1998, p. 264). When indirectly forgiving, the forgiver uses tactics such as humor, nonverbal displays (e.g. hugs, eye contact), or acting "back to normal" around the transgressor. Indirect forgiveness is believed to be conflict minimization strategy, used when "preservation of the relationship is more important than rectifying the relational transgression" (Waldron & Kelley, 2005, p.738).

The third way individuals forgive is with conditions. When forgiving with conditions (referred to here as conditional forgiveness), individuals tell the transgressors he or she is forgiven, but with stipulations attached. For example, one respondent in Kelley's

(1998) study stated she forgave her partner, but added, "we both knew that there was the stipulation that he stay off the booze" (p.264). Conditional forgiveness is used when individuals desire relational repair yet want to make it explicitly clear to transgressors that repeated behavior will not be tolerated (Waldron & Kelley, 2005).

Consistent with Kelley (1998), Waldron and Kelley (2005) found direct forgiveness (which was split into two categories called discussion and explicit forgiveness) was the most frequently used forgiveness type. Counter to Kelley, however, Waldron and Kelley found conditional forgiveness was the second most commonly used type, far ahead of indirect forgiveness (composed of two categories, minimizing and nonverbal display). It is predicted in this study that direct forgiveness will again be the most frequently reported type of forgiveness across the relational forms. However, because the studies reported inconsistent findings regarding the relative commonness of indirect and conditional forgiveness, a research question is posed regarding the frequencies of these forgiveness types.

Stanford University is the home of likely the largest intervention study on interpersonal forgiveness. The Stanford Forgiveness Project, funded by the John Templeton Foundation, is evaluating a six-session 90-minute forgiveness training program. This program was developed from a dissertation study. The study showed that normal college students could become significantly less angry and hurt, feel more hopeful, spiritually content and self-efficacious about managing their emotions and become more forgiving after a six-hour training session. Moreover, the psychosocial gains were stable over a ten-week follow-up period.

Later, another Stanford University professor of Education, Carl Thoresen, PhD, measured the effects of forgiveness training in a broader range of psychological variables and some physiological variables as well. They looked at the influences, if any, which religious affiliation and spiritual practices such as prayer and meditation might have on the participant's willingness and ability to forgive. The training was done with a group of twelve to fifteen participants, with the use of lecture, discussion, guided imagery and homework practice.

Studies have been conducted with adolescents who felt neglected by their parents, with women who were abused as children, with elderly women who felt hurt or uncared for, with males who disagreed with their female partners' decisions to have abortions and with college students who had been hurt. These studies showed that when given forgiveness training of varying lengths and intensities, participants could become less hurt and become more able to forgive their offenders.

One explanation for why forgiveness may be beneficial for physical health is that it deepens and promotes interpersonal relationships. Another possibility is that forgiveness is a form of religious expression or may be an indication of a positive spiritual experience. Studies showed that social support can decrease mortality rate. There is also a group of studies that demonstrate that people who have strong religious affiliations, or use religious coping, have decreased mortality.

Forgiveness may be viewed as an analogous example of the ability to see one's life through a positive or healing lens. While the research is only suggestive, it may be that all of us could benefit from training in managing life's inevitable hurts and using forgiveness to make peace with the past. In this way, forgiveness may be, as the religious traditions have been claiming all along, a rich path to greater peace and understanding that also has both psychological and physiological value (Luskin).

Chapter 15

The Power of Forgiveness in Marriage

We learn to honor God with our heart and not just our mouth. We are lying when we say we have forgiven but unforgiveness still rots our souls. Satan grips and weakens us through unforgiveness. He tightens his grip through a religious spirit that says the right things while refusing to confront the offense and heal (Meyer).

For a marriage to be successful, there also needs to be forgiveness. Repentance and forgiveness are complementary gospel principles, and both are necessary for us to progress spiritually. Resentment is one of the worst poisons in marriage. It does not ruin a marriage overnight. Rather, it is like a decay that gradually and silently damages your teeth; however, numerous instances of neglect over many years will. Similarly, resentment accumulates gradually, often without us even noticing it. If left untreated, it builds up over several years to the point where it destroys love.

Just as our sins and weaknesses are washed away through repentance, forgiveness washes away the hurts and emotional injuries that must be anticipated in being married to someone who is imperfect. Forgiveness is the perfect antidote for the poison of resentment. It neutralizes our hurt feelings and makes room in our hearts for love to flourish and grow. President Packer of the Quorum of the Twelve Apostles says that we all carry excess baggage around from time to time, but the wisest one does not carry it long. He says stop carrying petty and stupid things. Get rid of it. That is called forgiveness. It is a spiritual medicine (Miller).

These same principles apply within a marriage, and perhaps more so. President Packer said you must get over it and not allow hurt to clutter your minds and hearts. He says marriage is too important to allow people's weaknesses and faults to destroy a marriage. We need to forget and move on.

Recent studies have shown that forgiveness is an essential component of successful romantic relationships. In fact, the capacity to seek and grant forgiveness is one of the most significant factors contributing to marital satisfaction and a lifetime of love.

Forgiving yourself and others is about being willing to acknowledge that you are capable of being wounded. It also means that you are willing to step out from the role of victim and take charge of your life. Couples who practice forgiveness can rid themselves of the toxic hurt and shame that holds them back from feeling connected to each other. This practiced skill will allow couples to fully process and move on from negative emotional events, and ultimately create a stronger bond (Packer).

Often people equate forgiveness with weakness and it is widely believed that if you forgive someone, you are condoning or excusing their behavior. However, in marriage, forgiveness is strength because it shows you are capable of goodwill toward your partner. Studies indicate that forgiving someone is one way of letting go so that you can heal and move on with your life (Packer). Forgiveness is about giving yourself, your children, and partner the kind of future you and they deserve unhampered by hurt and anger. It is about choosing to live a life wherein the other does not have power over you and you are not dominated by unresolved bitterness and resentment (Gottman).

Forgiveness has been proven beneficial to a range of relationships, whether it is a family, romantic, or professional relationship. Forgiveness within close relationships is not harder or easier than forgiving absent individuals, such as strangers who rob or assault us or people who have moved away or died since hurting us. In ongoing relationships, forgiveness is simply different. A present partner can make things better or worse. An absent person cannot be confronted, but also cannot reject a confrontation or compound harms with new hurts (Gottman).

Researchers say people are usually more willing to forgive if they sense trust and willingness to sacrifice from their partner. They also predicted that forgiving would be associated with greater well-being, especially in relationships that are strongly committed rather than weak. They figured that people in highly committed relationships have more to lose if the relationship fails and so would be willing to make certain sacrifices. They used several methods, such as having people fill out questionnaires, recall past relationships, and assess their present relationships. What they found was that if people were unwilling to sacrifice at times, if they wanted to exact revenge rather than practice forgiveness, they often suffered conflict, negative emotions, and poor abilities to compromise when inevitable differences arose (Worthington).

The researchers also found that the relationship between forgiveness and well-being in marriages was stronger than in other relationships. Their findings suggest that the more we invest in a relationship, the more we need a repertoire of good strategies to guide it through troubled times, and the more these strategies will prove satisfying and rewarding (Worthington).

The researchers developed a scale to measure forgiveness between people. They asked people to remember a specific offense in which someone harmed them, and then asked about their motives for revenge and for avoiding the perpetrator. They found that people who showed high motivations for revenge and avoidance had lower relationship satisfaction. People who tended to forgive reported greater relationship quality and greater commitment to relationships (Worthington).

Frank Fincham and some colleagues reviewed seventeen empirical studies on forgiveness in relationships. The studies suggest that when partners hurt each other, there is often a shift in their goals for their relationship. They might have previously professed undying love and worked hard to cooperate with their partner, but if this partner betrays them, suddenly they become more competitive. They focus on getting even and keeping score instead of enjoying each other. They concentrate on not losing arguments rather than on compromise. They use past transgressions to remind the partner of his or her failings. Forgiveness, assert Fincham and his colleagues, can help restore more benevolent and cooperative goals to relationships.

Forgiveness researchers suggest that when couples and families fail to forgive, unequal relationships are created and maintained. True closeness is an impossibility because the "offended" is in a position holding the "offender" in bondage, and the obsession with being wronged and seeking revenge holds the victim in bondage as well. The person who made the mistake or hurt the other is kept in a "one down" position of being indebted to the other (Rowden & Davis).

It is important to consider that forgiveness is a gift you give yourself. Moskovitch (2014) reiterates that forgiveness is not letting someone off the hook. She writes, "Forgiveness is not the same as forgetting what happened, or condoning your ex-spouse's actions, giving up claims to a fair settlement or reconciliation. While forgiveness may help others, it first and foremost can help you."

Forgiveness is never easy, and forgiving an ex-spouse or to move toward forgiving, one must see the value of forgiveness in forging a new life, understand what forgiveness means, and see forgiveness as a process that will take time. All these steps will help the person change their actions and develop new habits and ways to cope with change and possibly see change as an opportunity (McCann).

We realize that some serious offenses are difficult to overcome, and some hurt runs deep. Sometimes a spouse has a difficult time forgiving something that others might consider trivial. In other cases, the level of resentment reaches a point where the spouse is unable to forget about it and move on with the relationship. In these situations, we need to rely on the healing power of the Savior's Atonement. His Atonement not only allows us to repent of our sins; it also heals those who suffer and grieve. During the process of the Atonement, the Savior suffered all of the pain, sorrow, and grief that we will experience in this life. Because of His atoning sacrifice, He shoulders the pain that we experience, which gives us the ability to overcome these hurts and to heal and forgive our spouse. The Atonement not only benefits the sinner but also benefits those sinned against that are the victims. By forgiving 'those who trespass against us' (Joseph Smith Translation, Matthew 6:13), the Atonement brings a measure of peace and comfort to those who have been innocently victimized by the sins of others. The basic source for the healing of the soul is the Atonement of Jesus Christ (Miller).

There will be situations where forgiveness does not mean staying in a relationship that is abusive or dangerous. There are some scenarios where divorce may be the proper choice. But even in these cases, the Atonement can bring personal healing.

We must be willing to take responsibility for our own sins and weaknesses that create stress and pain in our marriages. May we use the power of the Atonement to allow the Savior to heal our hurts and sorrows to help us fully forgive our spouses. The Savior not only heals broken souls; He also heals broken hearts. If we allow Him to help us sincerely repent and freely forgive, our lives and our marriage will be blessed throughout eternity (Miller).

Repentance and forgiveness are complementary gospel principles. Both invite the healing power of the Atonement to wash over us so that we can maintain peace and harmony in our marriage. Just as our sins and weaknesses are washed away through repentance, forgiveness washes away the hurts and emotional injuries that must be anticipated in being married to someone who is imperfect (Miller).

Chapter 16

Identifying Our Real Enemies

Domeniek L. Harris, a writer of *Today's Christian Woman*, (2013) says too often in marriage when there is offense and conflict; we identify our mates as the enemy. Our mates are never the enemy. If we learn who our enemies really are, we can effectively fight the battles in our marriages and rise to victory. Our real enemies are the power of darkness and our flesh. These enemies often go unnoticed in the heat of battle. Our flesh seeks to please itself and cannot please God. The apostle Paul warns us about our flesh, in Romans 8:8, "Those who are still under the control of their sinful nature can never please God."

The powers of darkness intend for all marriage to be destroyed. If you commit to God and your mate, you will wrestle with the forces of darkness. Ephesians 6:12 declares, "For we are not fighting against flesh and blood enemies, but against evil rulers and authorities of the unseen world, against mighty powers in this dark world, and against evil spirits in the heavenly places." When we can recognize our enemies, we are more effective in loosening Satan's grip on forgiveness.

Harris (2013) noted that something people equate forgiveness with something warm and fuzzy. Truthfully, forgiveness is quite the opposite. Forgiveness can be quite painful when it involves someone with whom you are madly in love. She said in marriage, forgiveness is not "Don't worry about what you did, I'm fine with it and we all make mistakes." It sounds spiritual and great coming out of our mouths, but inside we are struggling with hypocrisy. We are plagued by an abyss of pain, anger, bitterness, and resentment. These unchecked feelings can potentially become emotionally, mentally, verbally, or physically murderous. Forgiveness is not being so numb to pain that we are oblivious to reality. In marriage, when we embrace numbness, our hearts transform into ice. Forgiveness is not forgetting the offense. Forgiveness is choosing not to inflict the price for the offense.

Forgiveness is not easy, but we must understand that forgiveness was extended to us. Jesus said in Matthew 6:14-15, "If you forgive those who sin against you, your heavenly Father will forgive you. But if you refuse to forgive others, your Father will not forgive your sins." If you refuse to forgive, you operate in sin and in covenant with Satan.

We struggle to forgive because we justify our rights and inappropriately apply God's Word. Many of us have declared inwardly or outwardly, "The Bible said, 'Be ye angry.' We forget the rest of the Scripture verse:" '… and sin not: let not the sun go down upon your wrath'" (Ephesians 4:26, KJV). If we are honest, many of us are angry and sin for days, weeks, months, years. Many of us will carry the sin of unforgiveness to our graves (Harris).

Forgiveness becomes a struggle when we seek to please our flesh. We struggle because the Holy Spirit demands that we be like Christ. God is as displeased with unforgiveness as he is with sexual sins, deception, lying, and envy. We must remember that any sin any of us could commit, Jesus paid for at Calvary (Harris).

Elder Joe J. Christensen, an emeritus member of the Quorum of the Seventy, said in most cases, we are married only for a short time before we hurt our spouse's feelings. Whether our mistakes are intentional or inadvertent, we all end up doing things that hurt our spouse. He said in order "To develop a solid marriage, one must be able to admit they are sorry for mistakes we make… When conflicts in marriage arise, we should be swift to apologize and ask for forgiveness, even though we may not be totally at fault. True love is developed by those who are willing to readily admit personal mistakes and offenses."

Christensen says sometimes it is necessary to apologize more than once, especially if the offense is particularly hurtful. He said that over years he found that it takes several apologies before the sincerity of the apology can penetrate the wounded heart of an offended spouse.

Forgiveness researchers suggest that time must be set aside to discuss the issue one on one.

Repenting is important in marriage. It requires us to look inward, be humble, and take responsibility for our weaknesses. President Ezra Taft Benson (1899-1994) taught: "Think of the repentance that could take place with lives changed, marriage preserved, and homes strengthened, if pride did not keep us from confessing our sins and forsaking them."

The essence of repentance is trying to change ourselves in ways that will make us better people. On the other hand, the foundation of pride is the desire to cover up our own weaknesses and focus on changing our spouse's behavior. As we humble ourselves, we desire to improve our lives and take responsibility for our weaknesses. We must be willing to apologize and become better people, which is at the core of repentance. It is necessary for repentance and forgiveness for us to progress spiritually.

Chapter 17

The Power of Confession

1 John 1:9 says "that if we repent and confess our sins, God is faithful to forgive us." We need to remember that. The next time you ask God to forgive you and then feel guilty afterward, open your mouth and say, "God forgave me." There is power in the tongue. Praying and declaring Scripture out loud not only helps to renew your minds, it helps you stand firm, and it certainly puts the devil in his place. The devil will try to make us feel guilty even when we did not do anything wrong. We need to confess our sins until everything is out in the open and told, and then get dressed in our spiritual armor so we can firmly stand our ground.

It is only natural that we feel bad when we do things that hurt others or hurt our relationship with God. That is because we are intrinsically wired to want to be connected to God, our creator, and to one another because we are linked together in the Father's family. God never wants to be separated from us and understands our natural human tendencies. That is why God has given his people specific ways to repent from sin and Jesus instituted the sacrament of confession (CCC).

To experience God's abundant mercy and restore our relationship with Him, we need to open our hearts and receive the many blessings available in the sacrament of Penance. God has always called for confession and repentance. He wants to restore our relationship with Him. Despite our sinfulness, beginning with the first sin of Adam and Eve, God has always sought to restore our relationship with Him. Though "God created us without us…he did not will to save us without us. To receive his mercy, we must admit our faults" (CCC 1847). In committing sin, we exercise our free will; likewise we must exercise our free will to restore our relationship with him. The process of restoration has always involved confessing what we have done and repenting from our sin so that we may grow closer to him.

God gives his people specific rituals and ways to confess their sins. For many generations, God continues to reveal Himself and the ways in which He wants his people to live. In the Law of Moses, He also gave his people very specific rituals for confessing their sins. In Leviticus, the Mosaic Law provided specific instructions on how God's people must repent. They must confess their sin, they must perform a ceremonial act of sacrifice and penance, and they must use the intercession of a priest.

Confession reconciles us with God and deepens our relationship with Jesus. In the early centuries, Christians only approached the sacrament of forgiveness when they were weighed down with the guilt of mortal sin. Gradually a keener appreciation developed of how this powerful sacrament contributed to a Christian's spiritual well-being. So, while the necessity of confession for mortal sin continued to be stressed, the Church also encouraged its members to use this sacrament to deepen their loving relationship with Jesus Christ (CCC 1447-48). Christians realized that confession can increase true self-knowledge, uproot bad habits, purify conscience, prevent spiritual apathy, strengthen the will and provide the benefit of spiritual direction (CCC 1458, 1493).

In Matthew 18:21-35, Jesus tells a story of an unforgiving servant. In this parable, the King feels compassion, and forgave the man. However, later the man the King forgave refused to forgive one of his fellow servants. Therefore, we must understand that we forgive others, so that God will forgive us.

Sometimes Christians struggle with believing God's great plans for their lives. Do not trust your feelings. Trust God's Word. Jeremiah 29:11 (AMPC) says, "For I know the thoughts and plans that I have for you, says the Lord, thoughts and plans for welfare and peace and not for evil, to give you hope in your outcome". We must confess our sins, humble ourselves, and be patient and victorious in Christ.

The impact of forgiveness is that it brings increased happiness and health, with improved functioning of cardiovascular and nervous systems. It decreases overall illnesses, restores positive thoughts, feelings, behaviors, and promotes overall psychological well-being. It allows for more compassion, understanding and it reduces stress, anxiety, depression and chronic pain, and lowers the risk of alcohol and substance abuse. It promotes the ability to function better in career, education, work place, and gives an increased hope and optimism for the future.

Ultimately, the act of forgiveness releases us from past hurts, memories and enslavement. Alternatively, to not forgive is to surrender oneself to the control of others and allow the present to be consumed by the past. If we choose not to forgive, we subject ourselves to the possibility of carrying anger, bitterness and resentment into future situations and relationships, as well as depriving ourselves of the peace of mind, health and happiness we deserve (Hereford).

Chapter 18

Obstacles to Forgiveness:
Misconceptions or Fears

When harm has been committed, our inherent sense of fairness demands that the scales of justice be balanced. To forgive the person who harmed us or the one we love seems outrageous and inconceivable, contradicting our understanding of what justice should be. Some of the greatest obstacles to forgiveness are the misconceptions about what it is. But oftentimes the basis for rejecting the prospect of forgiveness is due to the numerous misconceptions. It is not condoning the behavior of a person. But once we understand that the act of forgiving does not compromise our moral standard by condoning the offense, we are able to forgive even the worst of sins. When we forgive, we transfer the person from our system of justice to God's.

Why Forgiveness Is Important

To forgive is to recognize that the wrong done against us is a debt of sin, and all sin is against God. Therefore, in forgiving, we transfer the debt from our ledger of accounts to God's, leaving all recompense in his hands (Arterburn).

Forgiveness is not ignoring or condoning (Gobodo -Madikizela, 2008); Enright et al., 1998), nor accepting or tolerating (Enright& Fitzgibbons, 2000). Forgiveness does not require accepting abuse and should not be confused with trust (Luskin, 2003). Forgiveness is not forgetting (Shriver 1998). Shriver emphatically states, "Victims of very great evil remember that evil for a very long time. We begin to forgive by not forgetting… to forget the evil is an assault on the humanity of the victims."

Forgiveness is not the same thing as a legal pardon (Enright et al 1998) as it is not connected to legal system. Because forgiveness is a personal response to harm, the victim may forgive the perpetrator even while the justice system takes its course. Therefore, forgiveness is not a way to satisfy the demands of justice; on the contrary, forgiveness recognizes that nothing the offender does could ever fully compensate for the harm they have done, especially in the case of traumatic violence. Forgiveness is also not reconciliation. While there is potential for reconciliation, it is not the driving force behind forgiveness (North, 1988). Forgiveness involves the response of one person, the victim, whereas reconciliation involves "two people coming together following separation" (Enright, 2001). North (1998) explains, "Forgiveness is an element in reconciliation, not reconciliation that is included in forgiveness." And in instances where the offender refuses to acknowledge their culpability and remains unchanged, reconciliation may not be a recommended or wise outcome (Enright, 2001; Enright et al., 1998).

Forgiveness is an emotion-focused coping strategy that can reduce health risks and promote health resilience: In *Theory, Review, and Hypotheses*, Worthington & Scherer (2003) hypothesized that unforgiveness produces ill health. In their examination of the empirical research, they identified four lines of evidence indicating that unforgiveness arouses negative emotions that could lead to physical changes like those produced in other stress responses. First, brain activity involved in stress and other negative emotions is consistent with activity in the brain during unforgiveness. Anger is the negative emotion that may be the link between the two, as it has been shown to have a high correlation with unforgiveness (Berry & Worthington, 2001; Berry et al., 2001). Second, hormonal patterns in unforgiveness are consistent with hormonal patterns from negative emotions associated with stress (Berry & Worthington, 2001). Third, Witvliet et al., (2001) found that sympathetic nervous system activity and EMG tension in facial muscles are like patterns found with stress and negative emotions. Lastly, blood chemistry measures show a similarity between unforgiveness and both stress and negative emotion. Seybold, Hill, Neumann, & Chi's (2001) correlational study of forgiveness disposition and physical markers found those who were unforgiving chronically had blood chemistry assays like those under stress.

Hostility, considered to be the core component of unforgiveness (Thoresen, Harris, & Luskin, 2000), has been linked to numerous health problems (Smith, 1992; Miller, Smith, Turner, Guijarro, & Hallet, 1996) to those of the cardiovascular system (Kaplan, 1992; Williams & Williams, 1993). Unforgiveness may also negatively affect the immune system. Under stressful conditions pro-inflammatory, cytokines, which among other things help fight infection, are elevated and this deregulates the intercellular immune system (Kieclot-Glaser, McGuire, Robies, Glaser, 2002) (as cited in Worthington & Scherer, 2003). Worthington and Scherer concluded that there is strong evidence to suggest that unforgiveness is stressful and that it can lead to negative health outcomes.

Forgiveness is not restoring trust in the person. Trust is earned. It is something we give to those who deserve it. To blindly trust someone who has hurt us is naïve and irresponsible. We can forgive people for the wrong they have done without extending to them an open invitation to do it again. It is foolish to trust an untrustworthy person.

Forgiveness is not doing the person a favor. In Judaism, forgiveness is not required unless repentance is demonstrated and pardon is sought. But Jesus raised the standard of forgiveness to a higher level. According to Him, we are to forgive even those who remain unrepentant. Forgiveness benefits the giver at least as much as the receiver, so we extend it whether the person asks it or not.

Fear can cause many of us to refuse to forgive others. It is the fear of losing the energy that anger produces. Some people are reluctant to let go of the burning energy that rage generates. It is like a fuel that keeps them moving. Without it they would likely descend into despair and purposelessness because their anger is their purpose. Fear can make us feel a loss of control in a relationship. We assume that if we forgive the guilty party, he or she is free to repeat the offense. Forgiveness does not guarantee change in the other person's behavior. Forgiveness is an act of obedience, not a tool of manipulation. It is a way of cleaning up the grudges and resentments that damage us. While we cannot stop people from hurting themselves, we can, in some situations, guard ourselves against repeated injury.

Some people fear losing hope for a better relationship. They place high expectations on friends and family and they let them down each time. Some want control and power over others through owed debt. Although forgiving feels like an act of surrender, those who have done it know it is an act requiring tremendous strength. When we hold people captive to our judgment, we play God in their lives. This places us in an unwinnable wrestling match with our Creator, who, as the apostle James reminded us, "sets himself against the proud" (4:6) (Arterbum).

Chapter 19

Healing the Whole

Ultimate healing comes from forgiving that person who wounded you. Your broken heart is healed by Christ as your burdens are lifted. Your soul finds rest in Him. Freedom and wholeness fills you as you realize you do not hold grudges anymore. You can look at this person with mercy and compassion now. They need healing that can only come from Christ moving powerfully in a person totally submitted to Him. You are released from the prison of unforgiveness which once enslaved you, finding complete restoration and deep healing. A load has been lifted and you feel much better. The memory remains without the bitterness. You know now what it means to "love your enemies and pray for those who persecute you" (Matthew 5:44).

Why Forgiveness Is Important

Forgiveness always results in your wholeness and restoration. God heals you. You let Him help you let go. We really will never fully grasp the depth of forgiveness (here on earth) and how it works in us as we forgive others. Forgiveness benefits us physically, mentally, emotionally and spiritually. Daily cleaning and renewal from God come when we confess, repent, and forgive.

We must walk in a constant state of forgiveness. Be ready to forgive before people offend you. It simply means we are ready to forgive because Jesus Christ forgave us and commands us to forgive others. We prove our love for Jesus by obeying Him. (John 14:15) Practice walking in forgiveness. It will change life! Move with His passion, love and readiness to forgive. This should be the mindset. Forgive! It is easier to forgive when those offenses come if you live like this. Despite the pain inflicted on us, no matter how wrong the offense, you and I must follow processes made easier when we walk in that readiness to forgive. You do not have to understand it. Do it and see what can happen. You will never be disappointed when you trust God. God's love and mercy endures forever. Abide in him and be ready to forgive.

When we refuse to forgive, have an uncaring attitude, or lack compassion, we will always pay the price for it. It is not, however, we alone who suffer. Our whole community suffers, and ultimately our whole world suffers. We are made to exist in a delicate network of interdependence. We are sisters and brothers, whether we like it or not. To treat anyone as if they were less than human, less than a brother or a sister, no matter what they have done, is to contravene the laws of our humanity.

If your own well-being, your physical, emotional, and mental health are not reason enough, if your life and your future are not reason enough, then perhaps you will forgive for the benefit of those you love, the family that is precious to you. Anger and bitterness do not just poison you; they poison all your relationships, including those with your children.

Let God heal you. Let His love flow over you. He knows all about pain and forgiveness. Healing will come as you let him carry you through your grief. His love is a consuming fire; it will burn up your resentments. Surrendering yourself to Him daily comes from abiding in Him. It is a continual process every day. We cannot bear fruit unless we abide in Him. The sinful self will interfere every time with forgiving and our growth as Christians. "He must become greater, I must become less" (John 3:30). This keeps us ready to forgive (Jayson).

Dr. Sam Von Reiche suggests several things married couples could do to help facilitate the process of forgiveness and healing their marriage:

State of the Union Meetings: Schedule regular times to discuss how things are going in important areas. Treat them like real appointments. Set times for both spouses to speak. Use the meetings for praise and support as well as for airing grievances. Keep them even when there is not something big to talk about. When these discussions have become a well-established habit, they will provide the best context to communicate effectively without fighting or withdrawal when something goes wrong.

Get Up, Stand Up: It is critical to stand up and take responsibility for the behavior(s) that caused your spouse so much pain, to express the simple but magic words "I'm sorry" with genuine sincerity, and then ask for forgiveness. Do not justify or defend the negative actions in any way. After all, who feels like pardoning someone when they do not seem to be sorry for what they did wrong, or are unwilling to right it?

Can Strike Twice: The final step in the healing process is to declare that you are clearly committed to protecting your spouse from future offenses. This should be backed by a concrete prevention plan. Without such a plan, history is likely to repeat itself and further damage the foundation of your marriage. If infidelity during frequent business travel caused the wound, for example, committing to searching for a position that entails less or no business travel may be an essential part of the plan. If you tend to become verbally abusive owing to a lack of good communication skills, purpose several sessions to work with a couple's therapist.

Living Out Loud: When your spouse openly solicits your forgiveness, respond by saying "I forgive you" out loud. You can go even further by saying "I love you unconditionally and commit to healing our marriage." These words are for you—not just for your partner—because statements of intention are very powerful ways to mobilize the subconscious mind to do WIT (Whatever It Takes) to achieve your conscious goals.

A Mile in Their Shoes: As a part of growth, both as a spouse and as an evolving human being reflect as deeply as possible on what occurred from his/her standpoint. This will take a great deal of willingness and humility because your hurt feelings will tell you there is nothing legitimate about what happened. But no matter what it was, it is possible to understand more fully where they were coming from to facilitate forgiveness.

Accept What You Can't Change: Learning to accept circumstances we do not have complete control over paves the way for forgiveness. It is also a key ingredient of wisdom and a happier life. If your spouse tends to be impulsive, over- or under-emotional, for example, he/she probably always will. It is the ongoing commitment to growth that counts, to work at managing and improving upon our flaws, and compassion rather than judgment from our partners that helps us to our feet when we stumble.

Only the Shadow Knows: Intimacy means you and your partner know each other intimately well. This includes situations where you are both stripped of the social personas you show mostly everyone else, and it is sometimes not a pretty sight. You get jealous. He gets loud. You are guaranteed to hurt each other with your "shadow "side.

For Better or Worse: When we take marriage vows to honor each other "for better or worse," we are not just talking about external circumstances. It is a promise to love our spouse unconditionally, for the best and yes, even for the worst, of themselves. This does not mean "loving them anyway." It reflects a commitment to love them, shadow and light together. Because it is only by reaching beyond the boundaries that separate us as human beings to embrace our common foibles and challenges that we experience true connectedness and meaning in life.

Chapter 20

Behavioral Benefits of Forgiveness

People are not required to be benevolent. Forgiving is a choice of behavior; an act of mercy toward one who does not deserve it (North, 1998). The choice of forgiveness leads to positive behavioral changes in the forgiver. Enright (2001) said that as feelings of bitterness and resentment towards the offender are reduced, the resultant negative behaviors (e.g. retaliatory or vengeful acts) are also alleviated. Genuine forgiveness not only diminishes negative behaviors toward the perpetrator, it also increases positive ones. Positive behavior may include the determination to no longer make disparaging remarks about the offender to others. It may be a smile. If the survivor is religious they may offer a prayer for the offender (Enright, 2001). A forgiving response to harm may induce any number of positive behaviors within the victim. Beneficial behavioral changes have been observed among severely traumatized individuals who have forgiven the offender.

In their study "Forgiveness as an intervention with incest survivors" Freedman and Enright (1996) assessed the effectiveness of an intervention program for incest survivors using forgiveness as the goal. The twelve participants were randomly assigned to an invention group or a waiting list control group. Pretests administered to the participants upon entering the program found the women to be anxious, depressed, and suffering from low self-esteem. Participants in the experimental group received one-hour weekly individual intervention sessions (based on the forgiveness model developed by Enright and the Human Development Study Group, 1991) in addition to a manual/workbook that described the process model and offered examples relevant to incest. Because each woman worked on the process at her own pace, the average length or intervention was approximately fourteen months.

After forgiveness therapy, all the participants in the intervention group forgave the perpetrator. A significant improvement in the intervention group's psychological well-being was noted as well as positive behavioral changes toward the abuser. As an outcome of forgiveness education, one woman returned to school with plans to start a business, one ended an unsatisfying relationship with a live-in partner; one went to see her father in the hospital and helped care for him, while another visited her father's grave for the first time (Enright, 2001). The horrific nature of incest and acts of violence and the commonality of negative psychological outcomes (e.g. PTSD, anger, depression, guilt, and low self-esteem) as a result, make it reasonable to suppose that forgiveness interventions would also be beneficial to victims and family survivors of violence.

British researchers Peter Woodruff and Tom Farrow suggest that the areas in the brain associated with forgiveness are often deep in the emotional centers, in the region known as the limbic system, rather than in the areas of the cortex usually associated with reasoned judgments. In one study, they asked people to judge the fairness of a transgression and then consider whether to forgive it or empathize with the transgressors. Ten individuals evaluated people in social scenarios while the researchers recorded images of their brain activity. Whether people empathized or forgave, similar areas in the emotion centers of the brain lit up. When those same people thought about the fairness of the same transgression, though, the emotion centers stopped being as active. This could be a clue for interventionists. To help people forgive, help them steer clear of dwelling on how fair a transgression was or how just a solution might be. Instead, it is helpful to get people to see things from the other person's perspective.

Research by Charlotte Witvliet, Nathaniel Wade, and Jack Berry, suggests other clues in encouraging forgiveness. They conducted a set of three studies that show that when people feel positive emotions toward transgressors, such as when they receive apologies or restitution for offenses, they experience changes in physiology, including lowered blood pressure, heart rate, and sweat activity as well as lowered tension in the frown muscles of the face. When experiencing positive emotions toward transgressors, they are also more likely to forgive them. Sincere apologies helped people forgive and calm down. Getting fair restitution on top of an apology magnified the effect. Insincere or incomplete apologies riled people up more.

It is important to stress again that forgiveness usually takes time. In fact, in a meta-analysis of all research that measured the impact of forgiveness interventions, Nathaniel Wade and his colleagues found that a factor as simple as the amount of time someone spent trying to forgive was highly related to the actual degree of forgiveness experienced.

Chapter 21

Physical Benefits of Forgiveness

The relationship between forgiveness, disease, and physical health is one that is being addressed in the burgeoning field of forgiveness research (Thoresen et al., 2000). The findings from studies examining the physical health outcomes of factors conceptually like forgiveness, e.g., anger, blame, and hostility (Booth-Kewley &Friedman, 1987, as cited in McCullough et al., 2000) have led scholars to consider that there may be a link between forgiveness and physical health outcomes. In research titled "The effects of emotions on short-term power spectrum analysis on heart rate variability," McCarty, Atkinson, Tiller, Rein, and Watkins (1995) conducted a series of studies which showed that an increase in positive emotional states, compared to negative ones, improved immune competence and reduced heart rate, blood pressure, and respiratory variability. Scheid (1996) said that there are twelve physiological and psychosocial mechanisms that provide an explanation of how forgiveness processes could influence health. One of these mechanisms works by decreasing chronic sympathetic nervous system (SNS) arousal which becomes activated for the fight or flight response, thereby reducing the demands upon the cardiovascular system (as cited in McCullough et al., 2000). Jiang et al (1996) found that people with higher reactions to emotional stress (elevated SNS arousal) were nearly three times more likely to suffer a major coronary artery event over five years than those with less reaction to emotional stress.

The physical benefits of forgiveness seem to increase with age, according to a recent study led by Loren Toussaint, a psychologist at Luther College, in Iowa. Toussaint, along with David Williams, Marc Musick, and Susan Everson, conducted a national survey of nearly 1,500 Americans, asking the degree to which each person practiced and experienced forgiveness (of others, of self, and even if they thought they had experienced forgiveness by God). Participants also reported on their physical and mental health. Toussaint and his colleagues found that older and middle-aged people forgave others more often than did young adults and felt more forgiven by God. What is more, they found a significant relationship between forgiving others and positive health among middle-aged and older Americans. People over forty-five years of age who had forgiven others reported greater satisfaction with their lives and were less likely to report symptoms of psychological distress, such as feeling of nervousness, restlessness, and sadness.

Hostility is a central part of forgiveness. Hostility also has been found to be a type of behavior that seems to have the most pernicious health effects, such as a heightened risk of cardiovascular disease. Forsaking a grudge may also free a person from hostility and all its unhealthy consequences.

According to a recent review of the literature on forgiveness and health by Michael Scherer, unforgiveness might compromise the immune system at many levels. Reviews suggest that unforgiveness might throw off the production of important hormones and even disrupt the way our cells fight off infections, bacteria, and other physical insults, such as mild periodontal diseases.

Chapter 22

Eight Keys to Forgiveness

According to Enright (2015) there are eight keys to forgiveness. It is important to know what forgiveness is and why it matters. Forgiveness is about goodness, about extending mercy to those who have harmed us, even if they do not "deserve" it. It is not about finding excuses for the offending person's behavior or pretending it didn't happen. Nor is there a quick formula you can follow. Forgiveness is a process with many steps that often proceeds in a non-linear fashion.

Working on forgiveness can help us increase our self-esteem and give us a sense of inner strength and safety. It can reverse the lies that we often tell ourselves when someone has hurt us deeply—lies like I am defeated, or I am not worthy. Forgiveness can heal us and allow us to move on in life with meaning and purpose. Forgiveness matters and we will be its primary beneficiary.

Studies have shown that forgiving others produces strong psychological benefits for the one who forgives. Forgiveness can lead to psychological healing, yes; but, in its essence, it is not something about you or done for you. It is something you extend toward another person, because you recognize, over time, that it is the best response to the situation.

Become "Forgivingly Fit." To practice forgiveness, it helps if you have worked on positively changing your inner world by learning to be what I call "forgivingly fit." Just as you would start slowly with a new physical exercise routine, it helps if you build up forgiving heart muscles slowly, incorporating regular "workouts" into your everyday life. You can start becoming more fit by making a commitment to do no harm--in other words, making a conscious effort not to talk disparagingly about those who've hurt you. You don't have to say good things; but, if you refrain from talking negatively, it will feed the more forgiving side of your mind and heart.

It is important to cultivate this mindset of valuing our common humanity, so that it becomes harder to discount someone who has harmed you as unworthy. If you practice small acts of forgiveness and mercy, extending care when someone harms you in everyday life, this, too, will help.

Sometimes pride and power can weaken your efforts to forgive by making you feel entitled and inflated, so that you hang onto your resentment as a noble cause. Try to catch yourself when you are acting from that place, and choose forgiveness or mercy, instead.

Address your inner pain. It is important to figure out who has hurt you and how. This may seem obvious; but not every action that causes your suffering is unjust. For example, you do not need to forgive your child or your spouse for being imperfect, even if their imperfections are inconvenient for you.

There are many forms of emotional pain, but the common forms are anxiety, depression, unhealthy anger, lack of trust, self-loathing or low self-esteem, an overall negative worldview, and a lack of confidence in one's ability to change. These harms can be addressed by forgiveness. It is important to identify the kind of pain you are suffering from and to acknowledge it. The more hurt you have incurred, the more important it is to forgive, or at least to experience emotional healing.

Develop a forgiving mind through empathy. Scientists have studied what happens in the brain when we think about forgiving and have discovered that, when people successfully imagine forgiving someone (in a hypothetical situation), they show increased activity in the neural circuits responsible for empathy. This tells us that empathy is connected to forgiveness and is an important step in the process.

If you examine some of the details in the life of the person who harmed you, you can often see more clearly what wounds he carries and start to develop empathy for him. You may be able to put an entire narrative together for the person who hurt you, from early child through adulthood or just imagine it from what you know. You may be able to see her physical frailties and psychological suffering and begin to understand the common humanity that you share. You may recognize her as a vulnerable person who was wounded and wounded you in return. Despite what she may have done to hurt you, you realize that she did not deserve to suffer, either.

Find meaning in your suffering. When we suffer a great deal, it is important that we find meaning in what we have endured. Without seeing meaning, a person can lose a sense of purpose, which can lead to hopelessness and a despairing conclusion that there is no meaning to life itself. That does not mean we look for suffering to grow or try to find goodness in another's bad actions. Instead, we try to see how our suffering has changed us in a positive way.

Even as one suffers, it is possible to develop short-term and sometimes long-range goals in life. Some people begin to think about how they can use their suffering to cope, because they have become more resilient or brave. They may also realize that their suffering has altered their perspective regarding what is important in life, changing their long-range goals. You must always take care to address the woundedness in yourself and to recognize the injustice of the experience, or forgiveness will be shallow.

Still, there are many ways to find meaning in our suffering. Some may choose to focus more on the beauty of the world or decide to give service to others in need. Some may find meaning by speaking their truth or by strengthening their inner resolve. If I asked for one answer, it would be that we should use our suffering to become more loving and pass that love onto others. Finding meaning, in and of itself, is helpful for finding direction in forgiveness.

When forgiveness is hard, lean on others for strength. Forgiveness is always hard when we are dealing with deep injustices from others. First remember that if you are struggling with forgiveness, that does not mean you are a failure at forgiveness. Forgiveness is a process that takes time, patience, and determination. Try not to be harsh on yourself but be gentle and foster a sense of quiet within, an inner acceptance of yourself. Try to respond to yourself as you would to someone you love deeply.

Surround yourself with good and wise people who support you and who have the patience to allow you time to heal in your own way. Also, practice humility, not the sense of putting yourself down, but in realizing that we are all capable of imperfection and suffering. Try to develop courage and patience in yourself to help you in this journey.

If you are still finding it hard to forgive, you can choose to practice with someone who is easier to forgive, maybe someone who hurt you in a small way, rather than deeply. Alternatively, it can be better to focus on forgiving the person who is at the root of your pain, maybe a parent who was abusive, or a spouse who betrayed you. If these initial hurts impact other parts of your life and other relationships, it may be necessary to start there.

Forgive yourself. Most of us tend to be harder on ourselves than we are on others, and we struggle to love ourselves. If you are not feeling lovable because of actions you have taken, you may need to work on self-forgiveness and offer to yourself what you offer to others who hurt you: a sense of inherent worth, despite your actions.

In self-forgiveness, you honor yourself as a person. This softens your heart towards yourself. After you self-forgive, you will need to engage in seeking forgiveness from others whom you have harmed and right the wrongs as best as you can. It is important to be prepared for the possibility that the other person may not be ready to forgive you and to practice patience and humility. But a sincere apology, free of conditions and expectations, will go a long way toward your receiving forgiveness in the end.

Develop a forgiving heart. When we overcome suffering, we gain a more mature understanding of what it means to be humble,

courageous, and loving in the world. We may be moved
to create an atmosphere of forgiveness in our homes
and workplaces, to help others who have been harmed
overcome their suffering, or to protect our communities
from a cycle of hatred and violence. These choices can
lighten the heart and bring joy to one's life.

Chapter 23

Choosing Forgiveness Can Be an Act of Empowerment

Forgiving does not necessarily mean forgetting, or even letting an act go unpunished, although for some people it does. We may forgive someone emotionally, but still feel that they need to experience consequences. Alternatively, we may still need to protect future victims. For our safety and wellbeing, we may choose to exclude the perpetrator from our lives or from society. Forgiveness means doing this peacefully, while no longer wishing them harm, wanting them to be miserable, or seeking revenge on others. Forgiveness is a gift we ask for and give ourselves.

Maya Angelou says, "Forgiveness is one of the greatest gifts you can give yourself, to forgive. Forgive everybody." Forgiveness can be a life changing experience and lesson. It allowed you to be set free from hurt, anger, and helplessness that keep us from peace.

Gandhi said forgiveness is an act of strength. You do not forgive because you are weak, but because you are strong enough to realize that only by letting go of resentments you will be happy and at peace.

Dr. Martin Luther King, Jr. "said we must develop and maintain the capacity to forgive. He who is devoid of the power to forgive is devoid of the power to love. There is some good in the worst of us and some evil in the best of us. When we discover this, we are less prone to hate our enemies. Love yourself enough to let go of all toxicity from your life and free yourself from the anger, bitterness and resentments".

Ajahn Chah "says when you forgive, you find peace; if you let go completely you will have complete peace. Peace of mind is what you find the moment you let go of any grudges and resentments you might be holding on to. As soon as you let go, you will find peace."

We depend on God for the grace of forgiveness. Attempts to forgive without the grace of God will fail because human resources for forgiveness are limited. Therefore, we must allow God to help us forgive. Becoming a person of compassion leads to becoming a person of forgiveness. We have within us the choice of good or bad. We have been and will be tempted.

Forgiveness is the key. Other sins can be present, and if your heart condemns you for something else, then of course, you do not have confidence before God. Nevertheless, it is a lack of forgiveness that most often comes between people and God. God has made it possible for us to know Him and experience an amazing change in our own life. Discover how you can find peace with God."

Forgiveness is the most powerful thing that you can do for your physiology and your spirituality. People feel that forgiving is associated with saying that it is all right, to accept the evil deeds. But this is not forgiveness. "Forgiveness means that you fill yourself with love and you radiate that love outward and refuse to hang onto the venom or hatred that was engendered by the behaviors that caused the wounds." (Dyer)

Forgiveness helps you live from your heart, not your head, and that is a key to embrace letting go of heartaches and feelings of being unworthy or unloved. Demo Di Martile discussed "Nine Fundamentals of Forgiveness." Cultivating compassion with forgiveness is an empowering act of love and a magnanimous expression of your spirits. Start with self and then others. Let go of your past and detach from pain and sorrow and focus on the pursuit of greater happiness. Choose to forgive and demonstrate your determination to right the wrongs, and bring about reconciliation, peace and harmony. Accept and practice forgiveness, nourish your soul and lighten your load. Love unconditionally. Love doesn't blame or find faults.

Love does not eject, judge, compete, divide, or seek retribution. Be willing to release your fears. Allow space for forgiveness to move into your heart. This healing is forgiving and soothing the pain of the past and eases the way to a greater peace of mind. Be liberated from injustices in your life. Set yourself free to soar to greater spiritual heights. Be peaceful by allowing yourself to be at peace with yourself, and let your heart be present every step of the way on the journey honed to the magnificence of you.

BIBLIOGRAPHY

Aldrich, L. Emmett. (2008). 10 Keys to Forgiveness. A Christian Perspective. *A Christian Response to Conflict Resolution.* Washington, DC.

Aponte, Dr. Harry J. "Love, the Spiritual Wellspring of Forgiveness: An Example of Spirituality in Therapy," *Journal of Family Therapy* (U.K.) February 1988. 20 (1), 37-58. www.harryjaponte.com

Ashton MC, Lee K (2005). Honesty-Humility, the Big Five, and Five-Factor Model. J. Pers. 73:1321-1353.

Ashton MC, Lee K (2007). Empirical, theoretical, and practical advantages of the HEXACO model of personality structure. *Pers. Soc. Psychol. Rev.* 11:150-166.

Battleson D (1997). Forgiveness as a factor in marriage and in conflict resolution following an extramarital affair. Unpublished dissertation, University of Nebraska.

Berscheid E, Regan PC (2005). *The Psychology of Interpersonal Relationships*, New Jersey; Pearson Prentice Hall.

Berry, J.W. "Forgiveness, relationship. Quality, stress while imaging relationship. Events and physical and mental health." *Journal of Counseling Psychology.*

Blair, Chuck (2017). The practice of forgiveness.
https://www.newchurchlife.tv/

Bettencourt, Feldman Megan. The science of
forgiveness: "When you don't forgive you release all
the chemicals of the stress response." Researchers are
studying how we can let go of our grievances and live a
healthier life.

Boon SD, Sulsky LM (1997). Attributions of blame and
forgiveness in romantic relationships: A policy-
capturing study. *J. Soc. Behav. Pers.* 12 (1); 19:44.

Brand, Rick. (2014). Forgiveness: The Forgiveness of
God. (http//: www.preaching.com).

Bugay A (2010). Investigation of social-cognitive,
emotional and behavioral variables as predictions of
self-forgiveness. PhD Thesis. Middle East Technical
University, Ankara. Turkey.

Canup, Linda. (2015). Forgiveness: Dr. Stanley
Explains a Vital Element of Our Faith.
(http://www.intouch.org/)

Cardak, Mehmet. The relationship between forgiveness
and humility: A case study. Psychological Counseling
and Guidance Department, Faculty of Education,
Sakarya University, Hendek, Sakarya, Turkey.

Cassity, Jessica. "Why Forgiving Others Is the Best
Thing You Can Do-for Yourself"

Close H.T. (1970). Forgiveness and responsibility: A case study. *Pastoral Psychology*, 21:19-25.

Coleman, P. W. (1998). The process of forgiveness in marriage and the family. In R.D. Enright & J. North (Eds.) *Exploring Forgiveness* (pp.75-94). Madison, WI: University of Wisconsin Press.

Cornell, Steve. (2012). How to Move from Forgiveness to Reconciliation. Millersville Bible Church, Millersville, Pennsylvania.

Chan, Amanda. "8 ways Forgiveness Is Good for Your Health" https://www.huffington.com/2014/10/25/forgiveness-health-benefits

Darby, B.W., & B.R. Schwenker (1982). Children's reactions to apology. *Journal of Personality and Social Psychology*, 43: 742-753.

Davis, DE, Ho, MY, Griffin, BJ. Bell, C. Hook, JN, Van Tongeren. DR., DeBlaere, C. Worthington. EL and Westbrook, CJ, (2015). Forgiving the Self and Physical and Mental Health Correlates: A Meta-Analytic Review. *Journal of Counseling Psychology*, 62, 329-335.

Deschene, Lori. (2017). "How to Maintain a Relationship with a Loved One Who's Hurt You."

DiMartile, Demo. (2016). "9 Fundamentals of Forgiveness: The Keys to Greater Peace and Happiness,", (http://onelightonespirit.com).

Dowd, E. Thomas, Ph.D., ABPP. (2015). Forgiveness and Reconciliation: What they are and what they aren't.

Dyer, Wayne. "Forgiveness: 5 Reasons Why You Should Let Go of Resentments"

(https://www.purposefairy.com/5311/forgiveness-5-reasons-why-you-should-let-go-of-resentments/)

Elder JW (1998). Expanding our options: The challenge of forgiveness, In: Enright RD and North J (Eds). *Exploring Forgiveness* Madison, WI: University of Wisconsin Press pp. 150-161.

Elliott JC (2010). Humility: Development and analysis of a scale. PhD Dissertation. University of Tennessee.

Emmons RA, Paloutzian RF (2003). The psychology of religion. Annu. Rev. Psychol. 54:377-402. DOI: 10.1146/*annurev.psych*.54.101601. 145024.

Enright, R.D. (2001). Forgiveness is a choice. Washington, D.C.: American Psychological Association.

Enright, R.D. (1996). Forgiveness within the counseling triad: On forgiveness, receiving forgiveness, and self-forgiveness. *Counseling and Values*, 40: 107-126

Enright, R.D. & C.T. Coyle (1998). Researching the process model of forgiveness within psychological interventions. In E.L. Worthington (ed.), Dimensions of forgiveness: *Psychological Research and Theoretical Perspectives* (pp. 139-161). Philadelphia: Templeton Press.

Enright, R.D. & R.P. Fitzgibbons (2000). Helping clients forgive: An empirical guide or resolving anger and restoring hope. Washington, DC: American Psychological Association.

Enright, R.D., Freedman, S., & J. Rique (1998). The psychology of interpersonal forgiveness. In R.D. Enright & North (E.Ds.) *Exploring Forgiveness*, (pp.46-62). Madison, WI: University of Wisconsin Press.

Enright, R.D., and the Human Development Study Group (1991). The moral development of forgiveness. In W. Kurtines & J. Gewirtz (Eds.), *Handbook of Moral Behavior and Development*, Vol. 1, (pp. 123-152). Hillsdale, N.J.: Erlbaum.

Enright, R.D., & Zell, R.L. (1989). Problems encountered when we forgive one another. *Journal of Psychology and Christianity*, 8(1), 52-59.

Enright, R. D. (2015). Eight Keys to Forgiveness: *Psychology of Forgiveness* University of Wisconsin-Madison.

Enright, R. and the Human Development Study Group (1994). Piaget on the moral development of forgiveness: Identity or reciprocity. *Human Development*, 37, 63-80.

Exline, J.J., Yali, A.M., & M. Lobel (1998). Self-serving perceptions in victim and perpetrator accounts of transgressions. Poster presented at the annual meeting of the Midwestern Psychological Association. Chicago, Illinois.

Fincham, F.D. (2000). The kiss of the porcupines: From attributing responsibility to forgiving. *Personal Relationships*, 7:1-23.

Fincham, F.D. "" Til lack of Forgiveness doth us part" *Handbook of Forgiveness* (pp.288-296). New York: Routledge.

Fitzgibbons, R. P. (1998). Anger and the healing power of forgiveness: A psychiatrist's view. In R.D. Enright & J. North (Eds.), Exploring Forgiveness, (pp. 63-74). Madison, WI: University of Wisconsin Press.

Fong, Ken, (2010). The Benefits of Forgiving. Collegiate Ministries.

"Forgiveness and its associations with prosaically thinking, feeling, and doing beyond the relationship with the offender," *Personality and Social Psychology Bulletin*, October 2015, "Forgiveness and Reconciliation" http://www.greatbiblestudy.com/forgiveness.php

"5 Steps to Forgiveness in Marriage" imon.com

Franks, A. Monica (2011). Struggling to Forgive: An Inability to Grieve, Excel at Life, LLC.

Freedman, S. R. and Enright, R.D. (1996). Forgiveness as an intervention goal with incest survivors. *Journal of Consulting and Clinical Psychology*, 64, 983-992.

Gandhi, Mahatma. Forgiveness. (http://www.purposefairy.com/7324/26-life-changing-lessons-to-learn-from-mahatma-gandhi/)

Gaspard, Terry. MSW. LICSW (2016). "How Forgiveness Can Transform Your Marriage": (https://www.gottman.com/forgiveness -can-transform marriage). *Journal of Divorce & Remarriage*, Independent Publisher

Gorsuch RL, Hoa JY (1993). Forgiveness: An exploratory factor analysis and its relationship to religious variables. *Rev. Relig. Res.* 43:333-347.

Greenberg L, Warwar S, Malcolm W (2010). Emotion-focused couples therapy and the facilitation of forgiveness. *Journal of Marital Family Therapy* 36(1):28-42.

Gumbleton, Thomas. "We need unconditional love, forgiveness at every level in our lives" April 24, 2015. www.ncronline.org

Hall JH, Fincham FD. (2005). Self-forgiveness: The stepchild of forgiveness research. J. Soc. Clin. Psychol. 24(5): 621-637.

Harris, AHS, Luskin F. Norman SB, Standard S, Bruning J. Evans S. Thorean CE (2006). Effects of a group forgiveness intervention on forgiveness, perceived stress, and trait-anger. J. Clin. Psychol. 62:715-733.

Harris, L. Domeniek. (2013). Today's Christian Woman: The Power of Forgiveness in Marriage, (http://www.todayschristianwoman.com/articles/2013/april/power-of-forgiveness-in-marriage.html.

Harvard Medical School. (2004). Power of Forgiveness-Forgive Others, Boston.

Hill EW (2001). Understanding forgiveness as discovery: Implications for marital and family therapy, *Contemporary Family Therapy* 23(4): 369-384.

Hope, D. (1987). The healing paradox of forgiveness. *Psychotherapy*, 24: 240-244.

Iyama, Chester, Forgiveness: By the lips or From the Heart? (www.gospelforumng.com)

Jacks, Kristin. (2017). Case Studies: "Forgiveness." (www.servantsasia.org)

Jackson, Wayne. (2017). "Understanding Forgiveness." ChristianCourier.com

(https://www.christiancourier.com/articles/887-undrstanding-forgiveness)

Jaeger, M. (1998). The power and reality of forgiveness: Forgiving the murderer of one's child. In R.D. Enright & J. North (Eds.), *Exploring Forgiveness* (pp. 9-14). Madison, WI: University of Wisconsin Press.

Jonah, Hieromonk. (2008). Forgiveness & Reconciliation: How to Forgive Others and Receive Forgiveness. New Jersey

Kachadourian L, Fincham FD, Davilla J (2004). The tendency to forgive in dating and married couples: The role of attachment and relationship satisfaction. *Personal Relationships*, 11:373-393.

Kalm, Von. Nils. (2014). Forgive and Forget: (https://www.redletterchristians.org).

Kaplan, B. H. (1992). Social health and forgiving heart: The type B story. *Journal of Behavior Medicine*, 15: 3-14.

Karremans, JC, Van Lange, P.A.M., Ouwerkerk, J.W., & E.S. Kluwer (2003). When forgiving enhances psychological well-being. The role of interpersonal commitment. *Journal of Personality and Social Psychology*, 84(5): 1011-1206.

Karremans, JC, Van Lange PA, Holland RW, Forgiveness and Its Associations with Prosocial Thinking,

Feeling, and Doing Beyond the Relationship with the Offender, *Personality and Social Psychology Bulletin*, October 2005.

Khoddam, Rubin. (2014). "The Psychology of Forgiveness." *Psychology Today*.

Kirby, Gregory. (2007). *Why Forgiveness Makes Sense*.

Kornfield, J. (2002). *The Art of Forgiveness, Loving-kindness, and Peace*. New York: Bantam Dell.

Koutsos P. Wertheim EH. Kornblum J. (2008). Paths to interpersonal forgiveness: The roles of personality, disposition to forgive and contextual factors in predicting forgiveness following a specific offense. Pers. Individ. Dif. 44:337-348.

Krejcir, Joseph, Richard., (2003). The Importance of Forgiveness, Schaeffer Institute of Church Leadership, www.churchleadership.org.

Lancer, Darlene, JD, MFT. How Do You Forgive Yourself? Psych Central.

Lawler, KA, Younger JW, Piferi RL, Billington E. Jobe R, Edmondson K, Jones WH. The Unique Effects of Forgiveness on Health: An Exploration of Pathways. *Journal of Behavioral Medicine*, April 2005.

Lloyd, Roy. & Enright, R. D. (2011). The Science of Forgiveness: Helping Clients Forgive, The International Forgiveness Institute.

Luskin, F. (2003). Forgive for good: A proven prescription for health and happiness. New York: Harper Collins.

Luskin, F. (1999). *The Art and Science of Forgiveness*, Stanford Medicine, volume 16 number 4.

Luskin, F. Thoresen CE (1997). The effects of forgiveness training on psychological factors in college age adults. Unpublished manuscript, Stanford University.

Markman, Art. (2016). How Does Forgiving Someone Affect Their Behavior: The influence of forgiveness on someone else is complex. *Psychology Today*.

Martin, S. Harold. (2017). The Importance of Forgiving Others. The Study of Matthew 18-21-35.

Marrazzo, Cortni. (2013). The Power of Forgiveness, (https://www.crosswalk.com)

McCann, M. Ellie., "The Importance of Forgiveness"

McCullough, M.E. (2000). Forgiveness as human strength: theory, measurement, and links to well-being. *Journal of Social and Clinical Psychology*, 19(1): 43-55.

McCullough, M.E. (2001). Forgiveness: Who does it and how do they do it? *Current Directions in Psychological Science*, 10: 194.

McCullough, M.E., Rachal. K.C. Sandage, S.J. Worthington, E.L. Jr., Brown, S. W., & T.L. Hight (1998). Interpersonal forgiving in close relationship II: Theoretical elaboration and measurement. *Journal of Personality and Social Psychology*, 75: 1586-1603.

McCullough, M. E., Pargament, K. I., & Thoresen, C. E. (2000). The psychology of forgiveness: History, conceptual issues, and overview. In M. E. McCullough, K. I. Pargament, & C. E. Thoresen (Eds.), *Forgiveness: Theory, Research, and Practice* (pp. 1-14). New York, NY: Guilford Press.

McCullough, M. E., Worthington, E. L., Jr., & K. C. Rachal (1997). Interpersonal forgiving in close relationships. *Journal of Personality and Social Psychology,* 73:321-336.

McCullough, ME, Witvliet VO (2002). The psychology of forgiveness. In: Snyder CR, Shane JL (editors), *Handbook of Positive Psychology*, Oxford Library of Psychology.

Meek, R. Katheryn. (2001). The Science of Forgiveness: The Center for Christian Ethics at Baylor University,

Merolla, J. Andy (2005). Communicating Forgiveness in Friendships and Dating Relationship.

Communication Studies, Vol. 59, No. 2, April-June 2008, pp.114-131, Colorado State University.

Meyer, Joyce. (2017). From Fear to Forgiveness, How to Follow Forgiveness Instead of Our Emotions.

Meyer, Joyce. (2014). How to Forgive and Let Go of Your Past: Importance of Forgiveness.

Meyer, Joyce. (2014). The Poison of Unforgiveness: Helping Yourself and Others to Forgive.

Miller, Richard. (2011). Repentance and Forgiveness in Marriage: Based on a devotional address at Brigham Young University. January 19, 2010.

Miller, T. M., Smith, T. W., Turner, C. W., Guijarro, M.L. & A. J. Hallet (1996). Meta-analytic review of research on hostility and physical health. Psychological Bulletin, 119:322-348.

Myers DG (2010). *Social Psychology* Ohio: McGraw-Hill Comp. pp 505-517.

North, J. (1987). Wrongdoings and forgiveness. Philosophy 62: 499-508. (1998). The ideal of forgiveness. A philosopher's exploration. In R. D. Enright and J. North (Eds.) *Exploring Forgiveness* (pp. 15-34). Madison, WI: University of Wisconsin Press.

Paloutzian RF, Park CL (2005). Handbook of the psychology of religion and spirituality New York: Guilford Press pp. 394-411.

Pettitt, G.A. (1987). Forgiveness: A teachable skill for creating and maintaining mental health. *New Zealand Medical Journal*, 100, 180-182.

Powers C, RK, Rowatt RC (2007). Associations between humility, spiritual transcendence, and forgiveness. Res. Soc. Sci. Stud. Relig. 18:75-94.

Radford, Nancy. (2016). Forgiveness: The Key to a Happier Future.

Rasmussen, Norm "Forgiving Others is Primarily for Our Benefit."

Reed GL, Enright RD (2006). The effects of forgiveness therapy on depression, anxiety, and posttraumatic stress for women after spousal emotional abuse. *Journal of Counseling and Clinical Psychology*, 74 (5): 920-929.

Reiche, Von. Sam. (2013). Give Forgiveness a Chance to Heal Your Marriage.

Richardson, Cole T. "Forgiveness: An essential in Christian Life."

Rusbult, C.E. Verette, J., Whitney, G.A., Slovik, L. F. & I. Lipus (1991). Accommodation processes in close relationships: Theory, and preliminary empirical evidence. *Journal of Personality and Social Psychology*, 60: 53-78.

Rye MS. Pargament KI and Ali MA, Beck GL, Dorff EN, Hallisey C, Narayanan V. Williams JG (2000). Religious perspective on forgiveness. In: McCullough ME, Pargament KI and Thoresen CE (Eds.) *Forgiveness: Theory, Research and Practice*, New York: Guilford Press pp.17-40

Sandage SJ, Worthington Jr. EL, Hight TL, Berry JW (2000). Seeking forgiveness: Theoretical context and an initial study. *Journal of Psychology and Theology*. 28:21-35.

Scott, Elizabeth, MS. The Benefit of Forgiveness: Why forgiveness? It's good for you. http://www.verywell.com/the benefits-of-forgiveness.

Seybold, K. S, Hill. P.C, Neumann, JK &DS. Chi (2001). Physiological and psychological correlates of Forgiveness. *Journal of Psychology and Christianity*, 20: 250-259.

Shapiro, R. Rabbi (2011). The Essence of Forgiveness: *Spirituality Health Magazine*.

Robertson, Pat. (2013). Forgiveness is the Key to Unlocking God's Miracle Power: The Importance of Forgiveness, CBN.com

Sherwood, Lacey. (2017)." Self-Forgiveness Is Essential for Healing."

Sifferlin, Alexandra, (2016). Forgiving Other People Is Good for Your Health, *Journal of Health Psychology*. Time.com

Shiota MN, Campos B. Keltner D, Hertenstein MJ, Philippot P (2004). Positive emotion and the regulation of interpersonal relationships. In: Feldman RS (Eds), The regulation of emotion, Mahwah, NJ, US: Lawrence Erlbaum Associates Publishers pp. 127-155.

"Six Important Facts about Forgiveness" *Psychology Today* 6/29/2015

Smedes, L. B. (1984). Forgive and Forget: Healing the hurts we don't deserve. San Francisco: Harper.

Smedes, L. B. (1997). Stations on the journey from forgiveness to hope. In Worthington (Ed.) Dimensions of forgiveness: Psychological research and theological perspectives (pp. 193-317). Philadelphia, PA: Templeton Press.

Smedes, L. B. (2002). Forgiveness- The Power to Change the Past, *Christianity Today*.

Smith, T. W. (1992). Hostility and health: Status of a psychosomatic hypothesis. *Health Psychology*, 11: 139-150.

Spidell S, Liberman D (1981). Moral development and the forgiveness of sin. *Journal of Psychology and Theology*. 9:159-163.

Subkoviak MJ, Enright RD, Wu C, Gassin EA, Freedman S, Olson LM, Sarinopoulos IC (1995). Measuring interpersonal forgiveness in late adolescence and middle adulthood. J. Adolesc. 18: 641-655.

Sweet, Rose. (2001). Marriage: Forgiveness and Restoration, Focus on the Family. (marriage/divorce-and-infidelity/forgiveness-and-restoration)

Tangney JP (2000). Humility: theoretical perspectives, empirical findings and directions for future research. *Journal of Social and Clinical Psychology*. 19:70-82.

Tangney JP (2009). Humility. In: Lopez SJ and Snyder CR (Eds.). Oxford handbook of positive psychology (2nd Ed.) New York. NY: Oxford University Press pp.483-490.

"The Freedom of Forgiveness" Bible.org

Thomas, Gary. "The Forgiveness Factor" www.christianitytoday.com

Thoresen, C. E., Harris, A.H. S. & F. Luskin (2000). Forgiveness and health: an unanswered question. In M. E. Pargament, K. I. & C.E. Thoresen (Eds.), Forgiveness: Theory, Research, and Practice, (pp.254-280). New York: Guilford Press.

Tutu, Desmond. "Why We Forgive" 2014 March-April, www.spiritualityhealth.com.

Tripp, Paul. (2011). Five "Benefits" of Unforgiveness (Then the Better Way) Paul Tripp Ministries.

Trujillo, B. Kelli (2014). "Five Truths about God's Grace"

Trujillo, B. Kelli. (2014). "Freedom in Forgiveness"

"Understanding the Healing Power of Confession" Catechism of the Catholic Church.

Van Lange, P.A.M., Rusbult, C. E., Drigotas, S. M., Arriaga, X. B., Witcher, B.S., & C.L. Cox (1997).

Willingness to sacrifice in close relationships. *Journal of Personality and Social Psychology*, 72: 1373-1395.

Warren, Rick. "3 Reasons You Must Forgive Others" www.charismamag.

Warren, Rick *The Purpose Driven Life*, Grand Rapids: Zondervan, 2002

White, J Matthew. "Forgiving When It's Not Easy"

Whitney, H. (2011). Forgiveness: A Time to Love & A Time to Hate. Campbell, CA: Premiere Publication.

Weir, Kirsten. (2017). Forgiveness can improve mental and physical health. Madison, WI: University of Wisconsin Press, American Psychological Association.

Witvliet, C. V. O., Ludwig, T. E. & K. Vander Laan (2001). Granting forgiveness or harboring grudges:

Implications for emotion, physiology, and health. *Psychological Science*, 12: 117-123.

Worthington, EL "Forgiveness in Marriage," *Handbook of Forgiveness* (pp.207-226). New York: Routledge.

Worthington, EL Jr. (2000). Is there a place for forgiveness in the justice system? *Fordham Urban Law Journal*, 27: 1721-1734.

Worthington, EL Jr., Berry, J. W., Parrott III. (2001). Unforgiveness, forgiveness, religion, and health. In T. G. Plante & A. Sherman (Eds.), *Faith and Health: Psychological Perspectives*, (pp.107-138). New York: Guilford.

Worthington, EL Jr. & M. Scherer (2003). Forgiveness is an emotion-focused coping strategy that can reduce health risks and promote health resilience: Theory, review, and hypotheses. *Psychology and Health*, 19(3): 385-405.

Worthington, EL. Jr. (2004). "The New Science of Forgiveness": *The Greater Good Magazine*.

Worthington, EL (1998). An empathy-humility-commitment model of forgiveness applied within family dyads. *J. Fam. Ther.* 20:59-61

Worthington, EL, Jr. & M. Scherer (2003). Forgiveness is an emotion-focused coping strategy that can reduce health risks and promote health resilience: Theory,

review, and hypotheses. *Psychology and Health*,
19(3):385-405.

Worthington, EL. Jr. & NG. Wade (1999). The social
psychology of forgiveness and forgiveness and
implications for clinical practice. *Journal of Social and
Clinical Psychology*, 18: 385-418.

Wright, Greg. (2003). Forgiveness from the Heart: Are
Christians Obligated to Forgive Unrepentant People.
New American Standard Bible, The Lockman
Foundation.

Wright, Rusty. (2006). Forgiveness, Reconciliation, and
You and the Power to Change, Spirituality, Power to
Change Ministries, Cru Global.

About the Author

Barbara H. Cooks, Ph.D, is a native of Shreveport, LA and graduate of Huntington High School. An active member of Steeple Chase Baptist Church, she serves as a praise singer and Sunday school teacher. She taught at Caddo Parish School for 23 years and Right Step Academy for two years as a coordinator and teacher. She also worked for Steeple Chase Baptist Church as teacher and program coordinator and for Shreveport's Metropolitan Circles, Inc., as a mental health specialist and advocate. She served as a program director for the Welfare to Work Program for two years. She completed an internship at the Rutherford House in Shreveport counseling at-risk teens.

Happily married to Rev. Andrew C. Cooks, Sr., she is the mother of four children. Her favorite pastimes are singing, jogging, and working out at the gym.

She hopes that this book will impact people in an awesome way. It is her desire to help people to understand the need for compassion, love and forgiveness toward oneself and others. Forgiveness is the key to a fuller, happier life.

www.ingramcontent.com/pod-product-compliance
Lightning Source LLC
Chambersburg PA
CBHW060926040426
42445CB00011B/814